T0305669

The Dynamic Progress Method

Using Advanced Simulation to Improve Project Planning and Management

J. Chris White • Robert M. Sholtes

CRC Press
Taylor & Francis Group
Boca Raton London New York

CRC Press is an imprint of the
Taylor & Francis Group, an **informa** business

CRC Press
Taylor & Francis Group
6000 Broken Sound Parkway NW, Suite 300
Boca Raton, FL 33487-2742

First issued in paperback 2021

ISBN-13: 978-1-4665-0437-0 (hbk)
ISBN-13: 978-1-03-217974-2 (pbk)
DOI: 10.1201/b21295

Library of Congress Cataloging-in-Publication Data

Names: White, J. Chris, author. | Sholtes, Robert M., author.
Title: The dynamic progress method : using advanced simulation to improve project planning and management / J. Chris White and Robert M. Sholtes.
Description: Boca Raton, FL : CRC Press, 2016. | Includes bibliographical references and index.
Identifiers: LCCN 2015045185 | ISBN 9781466504370 (hardback)
Subjects: LCSH: Project management--Data processing. | BISAC: BUSINESS & ECONOMICS / Project Management. | COMPUTERS / Information Technology. | TECHNOLOGY & ENGINEERING / Manufacturing.
Classification: LCC HD69.P75 W4895 2016 | DDC 658.4/0352--dc23
LC record available at http://lccn.loc.gov/2015045185

Visit the Taylor & Francis Web site at
http://www.taylorandfrancis.com

and the CRC Press Web site at
http://www.crcpress.com

Contents

Foreword

"How long is it going to take?" "What is it going to cost?" "What did you base that on?"

Most project managers have heard those questions on a regular basis. We answer them based on what we know and the tools that we have on hand. It is our *best-guess* way of dealing with something really complicated. Then, we spend the rest of the project trying to live up to those commitments.

I have known Chris for many years now, and he has always had a fascination with estimating. How can you tell a swag from an educated guess, from a fact-based expert opinion? How can we use computing power to make sense of a swirling mess of metrics and variables, turning them into more reliable estimates? This book puts his life's work into words in an attempt to help you simplify complexity. The Dynamic Progress Method (DPM) is an important step forward because it runs countless calculations that help you establish and refine estimates in a way that is impossible to do by hand. However, I think that it is even more important that it forces you to think about estimating in a much deeper way. It makes you think about the details of what could happen and model that out. Just the act of going through that thought process means that these factors are on the top of your mind. And, a focus on *the things that matter most* makes you a better project manager overall. If you know that some on the team are less productive than they were a month ago, what can you do to change that? If you know that skill differences are impacting your schedule, how can you deal with that?

Estimating is hard. It may very well be the single greatest challenge with which you, as a project manager (PM), deal. When managing a large-scale effort, there is no possible way that you can be an expert in every task. Once your estimates are in place, how do you make adjustments along the way? The way that you deal with these things basically determines your value as a PM in your sponsor's mind. Think about all of the ways that you can fail to make accurate projections:

You can accept and work toward mandated deadlines. Hopefully, anyone reading this book is beyond this. It does not feel like the right thing for anyone to do, but absent a solid basis for making an estimate, accepting the boss's deadline is your default position. The DPM approach outlined in this book forces you to take a more detailed look at what estimates *are made of.*

You can pretend that you know exactly what will happen. This is perhaps the most common mistake. You offer exact estimates when a range would be far more appropriate. Unless you are truly clairvoyant, this probably is not the way to go—but it is precisely what your bosses will ask for. The DPM approach in this book makes clear how variable estimates can be and gives you a better sense of those ranges.

Finger-in-the-air estimating. Ask the team to give you quick, *off-the-top-of-their-head* estimates. Again, the DPM requires that you dig deeper into the details.

You can create estimates at too high a level. The DPM forces you to look at not only tasks in a granular way but also how lower-level components interact over time. Again, it forces you to think more seriously about what you are doing.

You can ignore the interactions between tasks. The DPM approach forces you to look at the impacts tasks have on one another and how they will affect your overall effort.

Ultimately, all of these elements in the DPM give you a better initial estimate.

Then, there is the question of "What happens once the project starts?" How do you adjust for the inevitable twists and turns that your project will take? The DPM gives you a real basis for making those decisions. It also allows you to look back on how things have evolved and keep adjusting—ultimately helping you optimize the result.

Estimates are the lifeblood of projects. They are how projects get funded because they help us understand costs—which are basically our investments. If you cannot understand investments, there is no chance of understanding return on investment (ROI). If you do not understand ROI, you often cannot get the project funded.

Pick up this book; use it as a reference, but really let the underlying assumptions and models sink in. As you apply the method, I am sure that it will bring you greater success as a PM, and it will assist you in helping each member of your team to be more successful as well.

Dave Garrett
President, ProjectManagement.com
Director of Digital Presence, Project Management Institute

Acknowledgments

The material in this book has been developed and refined over nearly a decade. We first and foremost thank our wives and children for their support as we poured time and effort into the research and development of the Dynamic Progress Method (DPM), pmBLOX®, and the writing of this book. Without their love and encouragement, we could not have succeeded.

We also thank the group of people who were directly involved in the Defense Advanced Research Project Agency (DARPA) contract work at ViaSim Solutions. They include the following:

- Spencer Dillard (key developer for pmBLOX)
- Dr. David Ford (system dynamics consultant for the development of pmBLOX)
- Daniel Kaufman (DARPA project director for the DARPA Small Business Innovation Research contracts)
- Dr. Jeffrey Riddle (key developer for the SimBLOX framework that was used for pmBLOX)
- Jessica Roberson (software testing and administrative support)
- Curt Sherrod (business development and contract administration)
- Chris Underwood (software testing and website development)

In addition, we have had the great fortune of meeting several people along the way who were avid supporters of our work and helped us immensely from a mentoring perspective, industry perspective, or user perspective. They include the following:

- Dr. Barry Bramble
- Dave Garrett
- Hylan Lyon
- Robert Mansfield (U.S. Air Force Brigadier General [USAF BGEN], retired)
- Chris Spivey
- Ron Stricklin

We thank Lara Zoble and Laura Oknowski at CRC Press (Taylor & Francis) for their interest in our work and the opportunity to publish our findings. We appreciate their willingness to work with us to make this book a reality.

Finally, we thank the person who started it all for both of us—Dr. Louis Alfeld from Decision Dynamics, Inc. (DDI). We met and worked together at DDI with Dr. Alfeld and learned a great deal about developing applications using system dynamics models and the Small Business Innovation Research program in general, which formed the foundation for our thought process on the work that is contained in this book.

Overview Summary

If the reader is in a hurry, here is a summary of the entire book in one page.

This book is completely written around the hypothesis that many projects fail or have difficulties not because of the skills or abilities of the project managers running the projects but instead because of the planning and management tools that they use. These tools use very simplistic models and methods. Because of the simplicity of these models and methods, these project planning and management tools are incapable of capturing the *reality* of the project and, thus, provide misleading estimates for costs and schedules. Once a project manager is managing the project according to these misleading estimates, it is extremely difficult for him or her to understand the true status of the project, which makes it extremely difficult to successfully meet the goals and objectives of the project. It is like aiming a gun through a fuzzy scope; the chances of hitting the target are very slim. The cause-and-effect chain can be represented as the following:

Simple methods...
　　　　lead to unrealistic models...
　　　　　　　which create misleading estimates...
　　　　　　　　　which cause project difficulties...
　　　　　　　　　　and result in project failures.

The purpose of this book is to introduce readers to a new analytical approach for project planning and management, the Dynamic Progress Method (DPM), which corrects many of the major deficiencies of current approaches, as well as to walk the readers through the first commercially available software tool that incorporates DPM: pmBLOX.

This book provides an overview of the research and motivation for this work (Chapters 1 and 2), a snapshot of the recent state of project management and issues with current approaches (Chapters 3 and 4), a description of the new simulation-based DPM approach (Chapters 5 and 6), and details on using pmBLOX to plan and manage and analyze projects (Chapters 7 and 8).

If this book is to be used in a course of study at the undergraduate or graduate level of college, additional content and exercises are provided on the website http://www.dynamicprogressmethod.com.

In addition, prior to reading Chapters 7 and 8, readers are encouraged to download a free trial version of pmBLOX at http://www.pmblox.com.

Authors

 **J. Chris White** was born and raised in Dallas, Texas, and is currently residing in Rockwall, Texas, with his wife and two daughters. He earned a BS in aerospace engineering from MIT (1990) and an MS in industrial engineering from the University of Michigan (1992). In addition to his role at ViaSim Solutions, he is currently an adjunct instructor at the University of Texas at Dallas and Texas A&M University–Commerce. Chris has published numerous articles in the fields of leadership, total quality management, Six Sigma, project management, strategic management, and simulation. His certifications include Lean Sensei, Six Sigma Master Black Belt, Project Management Professional (PMP), and Certified Scrum Master (CSM).

 **Robert (Bob) Sholtes** was born and raised in Chicago, Illinois, and is currently residing in Boyds, Maryland, with his wife, daughter, and son. He earned a BS in aeronautical and astronautical engineering from the University of Illinois at Urbana/Champaign (1986) and an MS in engineering and public policy from Washington University in St. Louis (1989). He has also been a special instructor at George Washington University and an assistant instructor and research assistant at Washington University. Bob has published several articles and presented conference papers in the fields of software development, simulation, and genetic algorithm optimization techniques.

We have been working together for almost 20 years on some of the modeling technologies and concepts that are presented in this book. We are excited to publish our findings and innovations from the DARPA research and development contract that funded a large portion of this work. We hope that readers find this material interesting and useful, and encourage the readers to visit the following websites that are associated with this book:

- http://www.dynamicprogressmethod.com
- http://www.pmblox.com

Authors

1

Introduction

There are some great project managers out there who are using the wrong tools.

J. Chris White

This book is written for project managers who have

- Been involved with large and complex projects (e.g., lasting many months or years, involving many resources, involving large budgets);
- Managed several projects that have been late, over budget, or both, even with the best intentions and best efforts of the project manager and the project team;
- Been given a start date and end date by upper management and told to make a project plan that *fits in that timeline, no matter what*;
- Established initial baseline project plans that became obsolete immediately after they were launched;
- Experienced frustration with current project planning and management tools that do not easily incorporate real-world variables;
- Had difficulty using the data within their project planning tools to defend and/or validate their assumptions and estimates; or
- Are looking for a *better way* to manage their projects and *tell the story* of how their project is progressing.

The motivation and rationale for the research and development work contained in this book can be summarized with the following:

- *Problem*: Despite good intentions, many large and complex projects are over budget, late, or a combination of both.

- *Hypothesis*: The planning tools used by project managers are based on simplistic methods and algorithms that inadvertently provide unrealistic estimates for costs and schedules, which can set up unachievable expectations and cause a domino effect of replanning and re-estimating and, ultimately, result in a project *failure*.
- *Proposed solution*: Harness the power of modern computers to more accurately and operationally simulate the allocation of resources to accomplish project work to provide more realistic, achievable, and defendable estimates for cost and schedule.

BACKGROUND OF RESEARCH

The work described in this book was developed through two Small Business Innovation Research (SBIR) contracts that were awarded to ViaSim Solutions by the Defense Advanced Research Project Agency (DARPA). The Phase I contract (W31P4Q-08-C-0044) was awarded in late 2007, and the Phase II contract was awarded in 2009 (W31P4Q-09-C-0169). The Phase II final report was submitted in early 2011. At the time of the publication of this book, pmBLOX®, Inc., the company launched from this SBIR project, is seeking Phase III commercialization funding through an equity crowdfunding website.

(If the readers are unfamiliar with the SBIR program, please visit http://www.sbir.gov. The objective of the SBIR program, which is overseen by the Small Business Administration [SBA], is to help small businesses develop commercially viable products and services while also perhaps fulfilling a specific need at a government agency. ViaSim Solutions has participated in multiple SBIR projects and is extremely supportive of the program. The authors highly recommend that every small business check out the SBIR program to see if there are suitable opportunities.)

The original solicitation from DARPA (topic SB072-006) called for the "application and development of advanced mathematics for Department of Defense (DoD) applications (DARPA, FY2007.2 SBIR proposal submission, p. 10)." This cast a very wide net for the types of proposals that might be submitted to DARPA. Business partners at ViaSim Solutions (the authors of this book) had experience using advanced simulation techniques in several different domains. The authors chose to submit a proposal that applied some of these simulation techniques to large-scale projects (e.g., DoD projects). The research hypothesis was that many project performance issues, such as cost overruns and late schedules, are due to the fact that the currently available project planning tools employ an overly simplistic approach to estimating the cost and schedule for a project. This estimating approach provides unrealistic and sometimes unachievable baseline project plans. Although there are plenty of *poor* project managers out there, our belief was that well-intentioned, skilled project managers would still have project performance issues simply because of their choice in the software that is used for planning the project. Consequently, the authors hypothesized that the cost and schedule performance for projects could be improved through the use of a new and improved approach for project planning and estimating.

Through the SBIR Phase I and Phase II contracts, research confirmed this hypothesis about current approaches, and ViaSim Solutions developed a prototype simulation-based project planning tool, called pmBLOX, that eliminated many of the issues that are found in current tools. We have named the resource-based simulation approach used in pmBLOX as the Dynamic Progress Method (DPM), and it will be explained in later chapters.

GETTING GOOD PROJECTS FOR THE RESEARCH

For the research for this effort, ViaSim Solutions solicited real-world projects from many different organizations. It was actually quite difficult to get a good set of example projects against which we could have consistent comparisons. There were several issues with some of the example project plans that were submitted. As a result, many plans were eliminated from consideration. However, because one of the goals of this book is to improve the readers' overall ability to plan and manage projects, two of the major issues will be discussed in this section for educational purposes. Project planners and managers should avoid these two problems if they want to have legitimate, defendable project plans.

The first and most common issue for why an example project was removed from consideration was the exclusion of resources (e.g., labor, equipment, materials). In these example project plans, the only information provided for tasks was the durations. With no resources in the plans, it is difficult to gage the adequacy of the estimates. Should a particular task take 4 or 10 days? Who knows? There is no information on which to base the estimate. This is actually a very huge risk: building a plan with no formal consideration of resources at all. In this type of situation, how can the project manager have any confidence at all with regards to the estimate? And, if there is any doubt in his or her mind, what information does he or she have to compare, validate, or refute with?

The second issue for why an example project was removed from consideration was the exclusion of dependencies between and among tasks. For many of the example project plans received by ViaSim Solutions, the project plan simply consisted of a list of tasks with start dates and finish dates (with a stated duration between those dates). For these plans, it was impossible to know how to order or prioritize the tasks if resource constraints occurred. Just because one task ended on March 31, and another task started on April 1, it was impossible to know if there was a connection between these two tasks. Was the second task waiting for the first task to finish? Or, was there some other constraint that required the second task to start on April 1 (e.g., resources not available, waiting for material from a supplier)? In extreme cases, not only were there no dependencies among tasks in these example plans, but also most (if not all) of the tasks were expected to be worked in parallel. The plan was just a list of tasks. Of course, this is unrealistic with the application of resources. As soon as they are incorporated, the project schedule would slip significantly to the right (i.e., longer). In one particular example from the defense industry (which was not used in the final data set), one project was moved from 5 to 26 months, representing a 420% increase in schedule when the resources were incorporated.

———————

RESULTS OF THE DARPA SBIR EFFORT

After reviewing 40 real-world project plans submitted for the research on this effort, ViaSim Solutions created a data set of 16 projects that included those from the fields of construction, information technology, defense, and product distribution. The smallest project was 3 months long, and the largest project was 3.5 years long. All statistics shown in this research are weighted values so that larger projects have more influence on results than smaller projects. This data set was used to determine the *current state* of project management for the purposes of this research.

Note: Only 16 of 40 example plans were viable for the purpose of this study. This is a strong indication of the poor state of current project planning. The fact indicates that potentially more than half of the plans that are currently used in organizations have insufficient information even to be able to judge their reasonableness. The 16 projects analyzed for this research project at least had enough information to pass this level of evaluation.

Based on the issues cited in the "Getting Good Projects for the Research" section in this chapter, several criteria had to be met for these plans to be used as the initial research data set:

- *The project plans must be in Microsoft Project®* (MPP format). To be consistent, a single tool had to be chosen to be compared against pmBLOX, and Microsoft Project is one of the most commonly used current project planning tools.
- *The plans must have resources that are allocated to the tasks.* If no resources were in the plans, it would be impossible to understand the differences with a resource-based approach.
- *The plans must have dependencies that are established among the tasks so that task priority can be ascertained (i.e., task 1 must be finished before task 2).*

Some plans did not have explicit cost information, but they were still used. For those plans, labor hours were used as a proxy for cost, and approximate hourly wages and/or salaries were used for the different labor categories. While this is not completely accurate, it did allow for consistent comparison across the Microsoft Project version of the plan and the pmBLOX version of the plan. Furthermore, because relative differences were captured and highlighted in this research, the absolute cost of the project was not as important.

Table 1.1 shows a summary of the results from the research. In the table, "Original Plan" refers to the version of the plan in Microsoft Project. Across all projects, the average duration was 495 days. The average cost was $1.975 million, and the average labor hours for an entire project were 20,485 labor hours (all labor categories combined). These average numbers from the original plans are shown in the first column of the table. The second column in the table contains the averages for the same metrics from the equivalent pmBLOX versions of the plans. The third, fourth, and

TABLE 1.1

Summary Results from DARPA SBIR Project

	Original Plan (Average)	pmBLOX (Average)	Minimum Difference	Maximum Difference	Average Difference	Probability of Being Late
Duration	495 days	762 days	−2.3%	120.4%	54.1%	62.7% (over 495 days)
	Original Plan (Average)	pmBLOX (Average)	Minimum Difference	Maximum Difference	Average Difference	Probability of Higher Cost
Cost	$1.975 million	$2.488 million	2.0%	1492.0%	26.0%	53.4% (over $1.975 million)
	Original Plan (Average)	pmBLOX (Average)	Minimum Difference	Maximum Difference	Average Difference	Probability of Higher Labor
Labor Hours	20,485	20,708	−11.3%	18.4%	1.1%	50.3% (over 20,485)

fifth columns show statistics that are related to the differences between the Microsoft Project estimate and the pmBLOX estimate. The last column on the right shows the probability, based on the normal distribution of data for that metric, of the pmBLOX value being higher and/or longer than the original Microsoft Project value. For example, looking at the duration results in Table 1.1, the simulation-based estimate from pmBLOX on average showed a duration that was 54.1% longer than the Microsoft Project estimate, indicating that the Microsoft Project plan was underestimating the duration by a significant amount.

Although not shown in the table, further examination of the project data showed that the underestimation by Microsoft Project appears to be proportional to the size of the project. Larger projects seemed to do worse than smaller projects mainly because of the compounding effect of the miscalculations across many more tasks. For larger projects (>12 months), the average duration was +59%, but for smaller projects (<12 months), the average duration was only +29%. For larger projects, the average cost was +29%, but for smaller projects, the average cost was only +7%. Essentially, the larger the project, the bigger the difference (i.e., larger underestimation by Microsoft Project). We can interpret this to mean that for larger projects, it is much more likely that the estimate provided by Microsoft Project (which uses a duration-based approach, the critical path method [CPM]) would be incorrect when compared to the more realistic resource-based simulation approach that will be described later in this book as the DPM.

It is interesting to note that for labor hours, there was not much of a difference: the average difference was 1.1%. The small average difference of 1.1% indicates that the project managers developing the plans in Microsoft Project have a very good idea about what has to be done on the project with regards to workload and resource usage, but the tool itself provides a very misleading result when it calculates the duration and cost for the project. The duration-based CPM (discussed in Chapter 4) used in Microsoft Project makes it look like projects can be done faster and cheaper than they can actually be done in the real world. This is very dangerous and represents a significant risk when the planning tool, which is trusted to provide a guiding answer, shows an unrealistic result because everyone goes by what the tool says. Imagine if a spreadsheet provides incorrect calculations. As a user, you are trusting that the tool will give the right answer. In fact, that is why you are using it. Why else would you utilize it?

EXAMPLE: LARGE DEFENSE CONTRACT

For demonstration purposes, the results for a single specific project will be described here. This example project was one of the larger projects in the sample set with a total estimated duration of 39 months by Microsoft Project. The project plan is from the defense industry, and it is for the development of a prototype sensor system that will be installed on an aircraft. Figure 1.1 shows the results of several versions of this plan. The dark gray bars are from Microsoft Project versions, and the light gray bars are from pmBLOX versions. The bars will be described starting with the top dark gray bar and moving downward.

The top dark gray bar is the baseline plan in Microsoft Project. It indicates that the project will run 39 months at a total cost of $13.1 million. This version of the project plan is unleveled (i.e., the resources are not leveled to limit them to work a typical 8-h workday). Thus, we know that it is an optimistic estimate because many of the resources are overallocated (i.e., scheduled to work more than 8 h/day).

To remove resource overallocations, the project plan was level loaded in Microsoft Project on a week-to-week basis (shown by the second dark gray bar in Figure 1.1). After resource leveling week to week, Microsoft Project showed a duration of 599 months. Clearly, this is not realistic at all. That is approximately 50 years, which is much too pessimistic. However, that is the result that was provided by Microsoft Project. Also, note that the total cost of the project remained at $13.1 million.

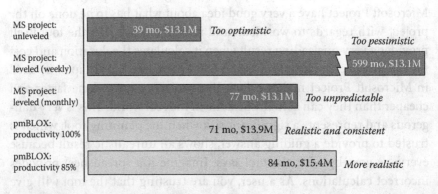

FIGURE 1.1
Example defense project for aircraft sensor system.

When the resources are leveled on a month-to-month basis (shown by the third dark gray bar), Microsoft Project shows that the duration changes to 77 months (with the same $13.1-million total cost). At this point, it is difficult to trust the results. Just because the duration of 77 months lies in between the optimistic, unleveled version of 39 months and the pessimistic, unrealistic version of 599 months, we cannot be confident that it is correct. It appears that simply switching from weekly to monthly leveling can create a huge variance. Consequently, these results are unpredictable. At this point, notice the significant difference between the three versions of the project plan in Microsoft Project. Depending on how the user sets up the plan, there can be very major differences. This situation represents a high risk because a *good* estimate is fairly arbitrary. Each of these three project plans has been calculated by Microsoft Project, so every one of them should be considered good. Yet, the plans are dramatically different. It is impossible to know which project plan represents a realistic and achievable estimate.

Figure 1.2 presents the project information for the five different plans in Figure 1.1 in a different form. Time is on the horizontal axis, and cost is on the vertical axis. For the Microsoft Project version of the plan that uses the week-to-week leveling of resource, notice the long, flat line that indicates that no work is being done from 2001 to 2047. No matter what changes we made to this version of the plan, we could not get Microsoft Project to show a week-to-week leveling version without this 46-year delay. It would be easy to *assume* this delay away in discussions about the project, but it is in the Microsoft Project file, so any information pulled from the electronic version of the plan would show this unrealistic delay.

Using the resource leveling function in Microsoft Project resolves the resource overallocations automatically, but the method is inconsistent at best, as shown in Figures 1.1 and 1.2. The same three plans were imported from Microsoft Project into pmBLOX with the assumption of 100% productivity for all resources. The results of all three plan simulations were identical: total duration of 71 months with a total cost of $13.9 million (the first light gray bar on the graph in Figure 1.1, which is the fourth bar on the graph). This appears to be a more consistent estimate. Standard project management tools, or at least Microsoft Project, tend to be either overly optimistic (when resources are not level loaded) or overly pessimistic (when resources are level loaded).

With pmBLOX, users also have the choice of changing the productivity of assigned resources. An additional simulation was run using a

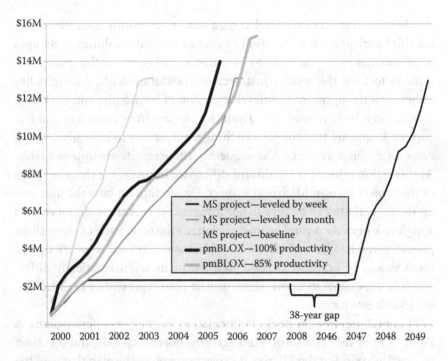

FIGURE 1.2
Another view of project information for the example project.

resource productivity level of 85%, which means that roughly 7 h of project work get done for every 8 h that a resource is paid. This is a commonly assumed productivity level for labor resources because it accounts for bathroom breaks, hallway conversations, and other nonproductive time that the employee is consuming on the clock. The simulation results from pmBLOX for this scenario are a duration of 84 months and a total cost of $15.4 million. When compared to the original plan in Microsoft Project (the first dark gray bar in Figure 1.1), these final results show a time difference of 45 months (115% schedule overrun) and a cost difference of $2.3 million (18% cost overrun). These are significant differences that are difficult to quantify and defend with standard project planning tools like Microsoft Project. The ability to bring productivity into the estimating process makes initial project budgets and timelines more realistic than those that are developed in traditional tools.

This brief example demonstrates that even the most experienced project manager can create a very poor baseline plan using standard CPM-based (duration-based) project planning tools because some of the underlying automatic calculations in these tools are inconsistent and, perhaps, even unrealistic. It also demonstrates that resource-based simulation can add a level of granularity that has never been achievable prior to the DPM.

BASIC ISSUES WITH MICROSOFT PROJECT ALGORITHMS (AND THE CPM)

The authors did not enter into this research project with the objective of criticizing Microsoft Project. Both authors have used the tool in previous jobs. But, since Microsoft Project was chosen as the tool for comparison based on its ubiquity in the business world, that is what seemed to be happening as the research effort progressed. This section highlights two very fundamental and very misleading calculations that were provided by Microsoft Project. Of course, other project planning tools that incorporate the CPM have these exact same issues. However, as stated before, since Microsoft Project was chosen as the tool for comparison, these calculations will be discussed within the framework of Microsoft Project.

Note: This book does not intend to teach the readers how to use Microsoft Project, so the following sections assume a basic understanding of the functionality of Microsoft Project.

Issue 1: Changing the Number of Resources with No Impact on Productivity

The first issue is a very obvious one. Microsoft Project makes a simplistic calculation for the duration of a task when the number of resources change. In this case, we will look at an example in which a single resource is used for a single task that is estimated to take 10 days (i.e., the duration of the task is 10 days). This is shown in Figures 1.3 and 1.4, which are screen shots from a basic plan that has three tasks. Figure 1.3 shows the task information in a table form, and Figure 1.4 shows the resulting Gantt chart for the project. All three tasks have the same duration (i.e., 10 days) and use the same resource (i.e., engineer). This is a very common way to set up a task in Microsoft Project, and these charts appear to be correct. Each task is set up as *effort driven*, which means that it treats the task work as a bucket of work *to do* that will get completed as the resource hours are applied. We applaud this approach because it is resource-based.

	Task Mode ▾	Task Name ▾	Duration ▾	Start ▾	Finish ▾	Predecessor ▾	Resource Names
1		Task 1	10 days	Thu 6/11/15	Wed 6/24/15		Engineer
2		Task 2	10 days	Thu 6/25/15	Wed 7/8/15	1	Engineer
3		Task 3	10 days	Thu 7/9/15	Wed 7/22/15	2	Engineer

FIGURE 1.3
Simple three-task project in Microsoft Project (table view).

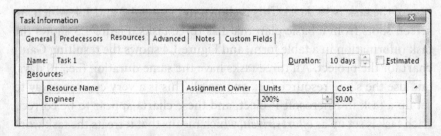

FIGURE 1.4
Simple three-task project in Microsoft Project (Gantt chart view).

Now, consider doubling the resources that are assigned to the first task. Figure 1.5 shows the input for changing the number of resources that are assigned to Task 1 from a single resource (person) to two resources (two people), represented by changing the *units* to 200%. Figures 1.6 and 1.7 show that the original duration of 10 days is cut in half to 5 days. The math behind this is quite simple. As in Figure 1.3, if it takes one resource 10 days to do work, and that resource is working 8 h each day (100%), then the task represents 80 h of work (i.e., 10 days × 8 h/day = 80 h). *Note*: Although the user did not enter a task backlog of 80 h, based on the other inputs, Microsoft Project *back-calculates* this 80-h backlog. When a second resource is added, as in Figure 1.6, now, 16 h/day are being applied to the task (i.e., 2 resources × 8 h/day per resource = 16 h/day). If we take the bucket of work to do of 80 h and divide it by 16 h/day, we get a new duration of 5 days.

Task Information

| General | Predecessors | Resources | Advanced | Notes | Custom Fields |

Name: Task 1   Duration: 10 day ☐ Estimated
Resources:

Resource Name	Assignment Owner	Units	Cost	
Engineer		200%	$0.00	

FIGURE 1.5
Doubling resources in Microsoft Project (inputs).

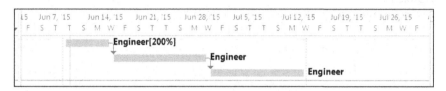

FIGURE 1.6
Doubling resources in Microsoft Project (table view).

		Task Mode	Task Name	Duration	Start	Finish	Predecessor	Resource Names
1			Task 1	5 days	Thu 6/11/15	Wed 6/17/15		Engineer[200%]
2			Task 2	10 days	Thu 6/18/15	Wed 7/1/15	1	Engineer
3			Task 3	10 days	Thu 7/2/15	Wed 7/15/15	2	Engineer

FIGURE 1.7
Doubling resources in Microsoft Project (Gantt chart view).

In this case, there is nothing wrong with the math. If we take those numbers and manipulate them the way we did, we get a new duration of five days for Task 1. The flaw in this approach is that the underlying assumption by Microsoft Project is that the resources do not suffer a loss in productivity, effectiveness, or efficiency when additional resources are added to the task. Essentially, each hour of work is treated as independent so that the total of the 80 h for Task 1 can be worked in any way.

In *The Mythical Man-Month: Essays on Software Engineering* (Addison-Wesley Publishing Company, 1975, ISBN 0-201-00650-2), Frederick P. Brooks, Jr. argues that throwing people at a late software development project only makes the project later, as current workers slow down on their work pace to help bring new workers up to speed, and new workers make mistakes (e.g., software bugs) that need to be corrected. While this may not always be the case, the need for coordination and reconciliation tend to increase as more people are involved in the same work task. That is the nature of most work that is done in organizations today. At present, hours of work cannot always be separated in typical projects.

Suppose that we give the benefit of the doubt to this doubling of resources. In other words, we accept the assumption that there is no change in the productivity, effectiveness, or efficiency of the two resources working on Task 1. Now, suppose that we push this to an extreme to make our point. Figures 1.8 through 1.10 show the results of allocating 10 engineers to Task 1 (i.e., 1000%). Unbelievably, Task 1 can now be accomplished in a single day. Suppose that we needed Task 1 in only 1 h. According to

Task Information

General | Predecessors | Resources | Advanced | Notes | Custom Fields

Name: Task 1   Duration: 5 days   Estimated

Resources:

Resource Name	Assignment Owner	Units	Cost
Engineer		1,000%	$0.00

FIGURE 1.8
Decoupling resources in Microsoft Project (inputs).

	Task Mode	Task Name	Duration	Start	Finish	Predecessor	Resource Names
1		Task 1	1 day	Thu 6/11/15	Thu 6/11/15		Engineer[1,000%]
2		Task 2	10 days	Fri 6/12/15	Thu 6/25/15	1	Engineer
3		Task 3	10 days	Fri 6/26/15	Thu 7/9/15	2	Engineer

FIGURE 1.9
Decoupling resources in Microsoft Project (table view).

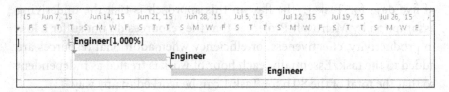

FIGURE 1.10
Decoupling resources in Microsoft Project (Gantt chart view).

Microsoft Project, if we assign 80 engineers to Task 1, it will be done in a single hour. Can you imagine 80 people working on the same task? This assumption of no loss in productivity, effectiveness, or efficiency eventually becomes farcical—perhaps not with two resources and perhaps not with three resources. But, eventually, the coordination and reconciliation factors will have a major impact. In today's business world, however, tasks are so interdependent that even adding just one additional resource to a task can cause a significant disruption.

In summary, with this first issue, the calculations and results shown in Microsoft Project are correct in the sense that the math is correct, but they are poor representations of reality because they assume no productivity impacts. Thus, this issue is dangerous from the standpoint of oversimplification and can easily lead to poor estimates for the cost and schedule of a project, even with the best intentions of the project manager.

Microsoft Project has no way to easily incorporate productivity differences or impacts, so this factor is simply disregarded. The users can work around this issue by playing with the units percentage to capture productivity impacts on work completion, but this will have cascading impacts on other elements of the project, such as the cost of the project and any earned value calculations. For example, instead of using 200% to represent doubling the resources on Task 1, a value like 150% could be used to indicate that two resources working together are only 75% as productive as they are when they are working alone (e.g., 2 people × 75% productivity = 150% units). This would provide the correct work completion rate, but the 150% in Microsoft Project means that 1.5 people are used (not the 2 people who we know are actually working). Since that number represents 1.5 people to Microsoft Project (instead of 2), the calculated cost of the task will be lower than the real cost (e.g., 1.5× versus 2×), which will impact other key metrics like earned value metrics.

Issue 2: Changing Daily Work Time for Resources with No Impact on Productivity

The second issue is not so obvious, which makes it more dangerous with regard to its impact on the cost and schedule estimates for projects. Let us consider the same three-task example that is shown in Figure 1.3. Notice that Task 1 runs from June 11 to 24, Task 2 runs from June 25 to July 8, and Task 3 runs from July 9 to 22. This represents a duration of 30 working days. We will now try to shorten the duration by making the resources work more hours in a day (i.e., apply overtime). By default, the Standard calendar in Microsoft Project uses a typical 8-h workday. In Figure 1.11, the hours per day have been increased to 16. In the background calculations, increasing a single resource to 16 h/day of work (1 person × 16 h/day = 16 h/day) is equivalent to doubling the resources working 8 h/day (2 people × 8 h/day = 16 h/day), as was shown with the first issue in the "Issue 1: Changing the Number of Resources with No Impact on Productivity" section in this chapter. Thus, we know that the new duration for the tasks should be 5 days (80 h of work/16 h/day = 5 days). This is shown in Figure 1.12 in the column called "Duration."

Similar to the first issue of no productivity impacts due to changing the number of resources assigned to a task, there is also a lack of productivity impact in this situation. According to Microsoft Project (and all the other tools that use the CPM), a person can work any amount during a

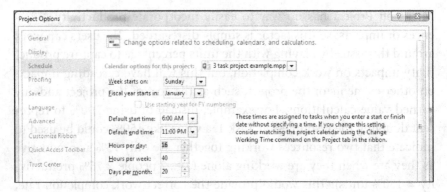

FIGURE 1.11
Changing workday hours to 16 h/day in Microsoft Project (inputs).

		Task Mode	Task Name	Duration	Start	Finish	Predecessor	Resource Names
1			Task 1	5 days	Thu 6/11/15	Wed 6/24/15		Engineer
2			Task 2	5 days	Thu 6/25/15	Wed 7/8/15	1	Engineer
3			Task 3	5 days	Thu 7/9/15	Wed 7/22/15	2	Engineer

FIGURE 1.12
Changing workday hours to 16 h/day in Microsoft Project (table view).

day (and for many days in a row) with no impact on his or her productivity, effectiveness, or efficiency. We can push this to the extreme and have the resources work 24 h/day (i.e., nonstop), as shown in Figure 1.13. And, as expected by the math, the durations for the tasks shorten to 3.33 days each (Figure 1.14).

Like the first issue, the math is correct: 80 h of work/24 h/day = 3.33 days. And, like the first issue, the lack of productivity impacts poses a major problem. It is totally unrealistic and can cause misleading estimates for project cost and schedule. Resources are treated as machines that can work nonstop with no fatigue or burnout. Yet, we all have probably experienced fatigue, burnout, and loss of productivity at some point in our working lives when we have been pushed beyond the normal 8-h workday for extended periods of time.

This issue is bad enough with the unrealistic assumption of no loss in productivity. However, notice that the start and finish dates in Figures 1.12 and 1.14 have not changed from Figure 1.3. They are exactly the same dates. This is extremely problematic. The duration for each task is stated as 5 days in Figure 1.12 and 3.33 days in Figure 1.14, but the *calendar* of the project still shows that each task is 10 days in duration. These are

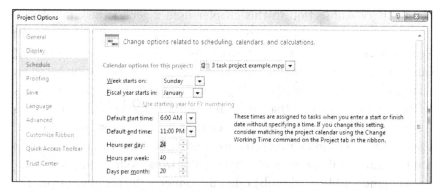

FIGURE 1.13
Changing workday hours to 24 h/day in Microsoft Project (inputs).

	Task Mode ▾	Task Name ▾	Duration ▾	Start ▾	Finish ▾	Predecessor ▾	Resource Names
1		Task 1	3.33 days	Thu 6/11/15	Wed 6/24/15		Engineer
2		Task 2	3.33 days	Thu 6/25/15	Wed 7/8/15	1	Engineer
3		Task 3	3.33 days	Thu 7/9/15	Wed 7/22/15	2	Engineer

FIGURE 1.14
Changing workday hours to 16 h/day in Microsoft Project (table view).

conflicting data points. Which duration is the *real* duration, and which duration is Microsoft Project using for other internal calculations that are unseen by the user? Imagine a much larger project in which the calendar for a specific resource has been changed to allocate that resource for more hours during a day, perhaps to act as overtime work to try to get a late project back on track. The results provided by Microsoft Project will be completely unpredictable and unreliable.

Issue 3: Ease of Use versus Practicality

This issue is not a calculation-related issue like the two issues that were presented in "Issue 1: Changing the Number of Resources with No Impact on Productivity" and "Issue 2: Changing Daily Work Time for Resources with No Impact on Productivity" subsections in this chapter. But, it will be highlighted because it is an issue that causes problems with cost and schedule estimates. In Chapter 4, the details of the CPM will be discussed. For now, what the reader needs to know is that the major input for CPM-based tools like Microsoft Project is task duration. The example in the "Issue 2: Changing Daily Work Time for Resources with No Impact on

Productivity" subsection in this chapter used a generic task that had a 10-day duration. From that duration, if a resource was assigned, Microsoft Project back-calculated the total work hours for the project so that this number could be used to calculate other changes in the duration based on changes in resource-related data (e.g., hours per day, number of resources).

The key point here is that the major input is the task duration. This means that a task can be solely represented by a duration, with no concern for the resources necessary for that task, even though resources are the real-world components that get the work done. Thus, Microsoft Project (and CPM-based tools) often disconnects the resources from the duration in an attempt to make the tool user-friendly and easy to learn. Now, users who are new to project management can quickly and easily put together a project plan. However, when durations are disconnected from the underlying resources, a huge risk is introduced into the project: there is no assurance that these durations are correct. There is no way to validate these duration assumptions. And, as things change along the way, it is impossible to know the impacts because each task is essentially just a bar that was drawn on a chart with no other related information. Microsoft Project even makes this explicit, as seen in Figure 1.15. Notice in the center of the screen shot that there is a checkbox option for "Scheduling ignores resource calendar."

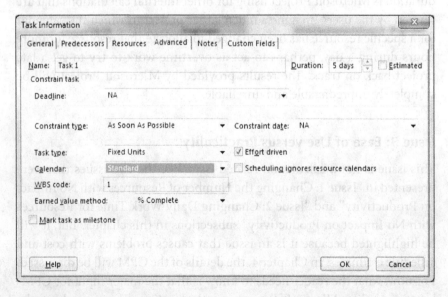

FIGURE 1.15
Example of how Microsoft Project disconnects durations from resources.

DIRECT COMPARISONS BETWEEN MICROSOFT PROJECT AND pmBLOX

As stated in the "Background of Research" section in this chapter, a major goal of the SBIR research project was to compare and contrast approaches that are offered by traditional duration-based project planning tools, represented by Microsoft Project, and a resource-based simulation approach to project planning, represented by pmBLOX. To do this, the authors compared common issues that are faced by project managers to see whether pmBLOX offered an advantage over current practices. The following sections describe two specific test cases that highlight some of these differences. The errors from these differences get amplified in larger projects because the errors can happen on each task. These are some of the reasons for the misleading estimates that are provided by a tool like Microsoft Project.

Test Case 1: Resource Availability

Microsoft Project

The first test case simply looks at how easy it is to account for a resource's restricted availability over the duration of a task. In Microsoft Project, a single task is set up to take 5 days, and is set up as a fixed-unit, effort-driven task (Figure 1.16).

A single resource (John Smith) is assigned to this task with the units available set to 100% (Figure 1.17). This results in the planned task being completed in 5 days, with John Smith working 40 h to complete the task.

What happens if, midway through the task, we find that John Smith can only devote half a day to the task? He is still working a full day, but suppose that other commitments limit the time that he can spend on this particular task. To model this in Microsoft Project, we adjust the resource availability to reflect this case, as shown in Figure 1.18.

This resource availability is not quite accurate because it reflects John Smith's total availability across all tasks. In other words, it is not possible to specify that for several days, John Smith will only work part time on this particular task. For this single task example, however, this availability does reflect his time that was devoted to the single task. Figure 1.19 shows how Microsoft Project represents this change in availability.

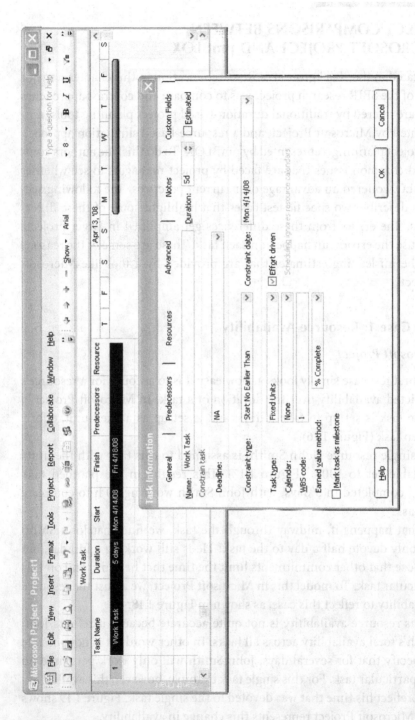

FIGURE 1.16

Setting up a simple task in Microsoft Project.

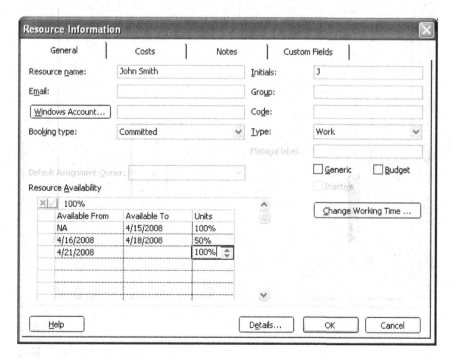

FIGURE 1.17
Assigning resources in Microsoft Project.

By default, all Microsoft Project can offer is a way to show that John Smith is *overallocated* because the resource was initially set up to work 100% of his time on the task. Resource leveling is one way to modify the schedule so that it reflects the reality of the resource constraints. However, when leveling is applied, the result is less than satisfactory. Instead of having John Smith work 4 h on the 2 days that his availability is restricted, the leveling algorithm simply ignores those days, and the total calendar duration of the task becomes 8 days (Figure 1.20).

FIGURE 1.18
Changing resource availability in Microsoft Project.

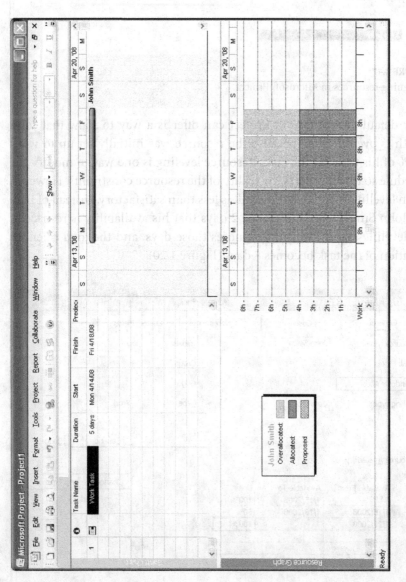

FIGURE 1.19

Resource allocation affected by resource availability.

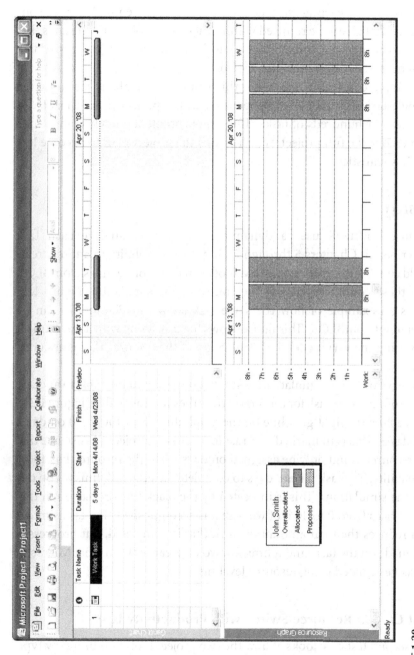

FIGURE 1.20
Level loading resources.

Worse, if John Smith is initially available at 100%, but is only available 50% of the time 2 days into the task, Microsoft Project is unable to provide any sort of leveling estimate (Figure 1.21). This seemingly simple constraint is not able to be resolved within Microsoft Project. The result is that the project manager ends up having to *hack* the solution to approximate what he or she expects the plan to show.

If simple constraint issues like this result in unrealistic planning for a single task, imagine what happens when the project manager is faced with tens or hundreds of tasks. This simple problem quickly compounds throughout the full project, which causes the project plan to become less and less realistic.

pmBLOX

Because pmBLOX uses a dynamic simulation to analyze each task (described in Chapters 5 through 7), it has the capability to address real-world constraints, like varying levels of availability on each task. pmBLOX uses these conditions during the course of the simulation. Figure 1.22 shows an example of how the same task shown in Figure 1.16 can be entered into pmBLOX. This figure shows the task along with a mechanism for setting the varying level of availability of the resource that is assigned to the task.

When this task is simulated, we see that the simulation is able to allocate the resource to the task for the 50% of time they have available (Figure 1.23). Notice how the light gray line on the graph dips from 100 to 50 on day 2 and day 3. This is in marked contrast to Microsoft Project's insistence that the resource could only be assigned on days when the resource has 100% availability. The task takes 8 days to complete (i.e., the task finishes on day 8 of the simulation). This is indicated by the black line on the graph that slowly rises from 0 to 40 h of work that is accomplished. The task simulation reduces the total amount of work that is completed, but progress is still made on the task, and it finishes two days earlier than what Microsoft Project estimated using resource leveling.

Test Case 2: Resource Switch with Productivity Loss

The second test case looks at how the two project tools handle a very typical problem. A resource assigned to a task is no longer available (e.g., he or she quits, becomes ill). A new resource is asked to take over the task.

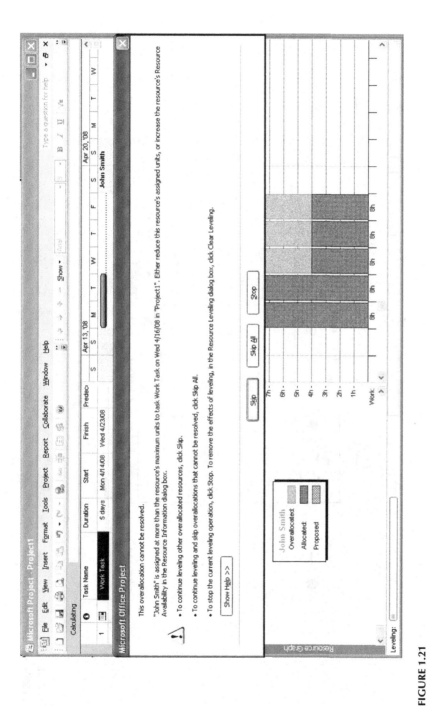

FIGURE 1.21

A simple resource constraint confounds Microsoft Project.

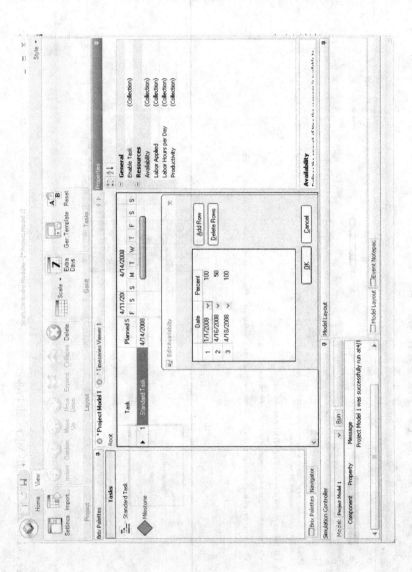

FIGURE 1.22

Task definition in pmBLOX.

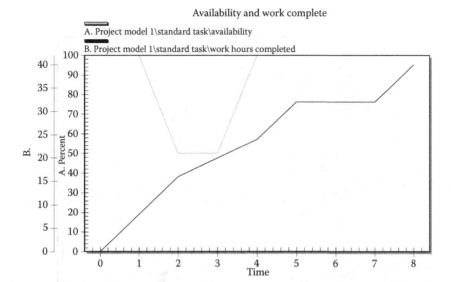

FIGURE 1.23
Simulating the work progress.

However, this new resource is significantly less knowledgeable and, therefore, will require time to ramp up on the task.

Microsoft Project

In Microsoft Project, it is very difficult to set up a task where two different resources will work on the same task, but one will be assigned only after the first resource has left. You could add two resources, for example, senior analyst and junior analyst, and define their availability based on the dates that the senior analyst is expected to leave. However, because availability is globally specified for the resource, it does not necessarily reflect that the junior analyst is available 100% of his or her time—just not on this task (Figure 1.24).

If the junior analyst is assigned to any other tasks prior to April 19, he or she will not be assigned because the availability is set to 0%. Clearly, this approach will not work. A second alternative is to manually go into the task and specify the hours that were worked by each of the resources, as shown in Figure 1.25. This results in a 10-day duration for the task.

This looks reasonable on the surface, but it is still fraught with error. For instance, the hours worked do not reflect that there is learning that is required by the junior analyst. With Microsoft Project, a project planner

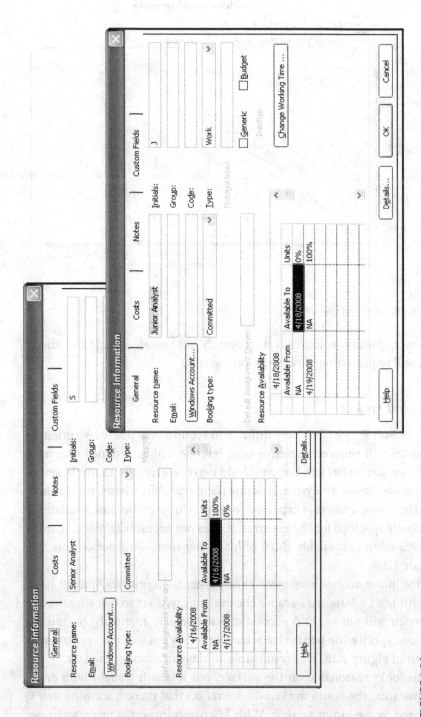

FIGURE 1.24
Specifying availability for the resources.

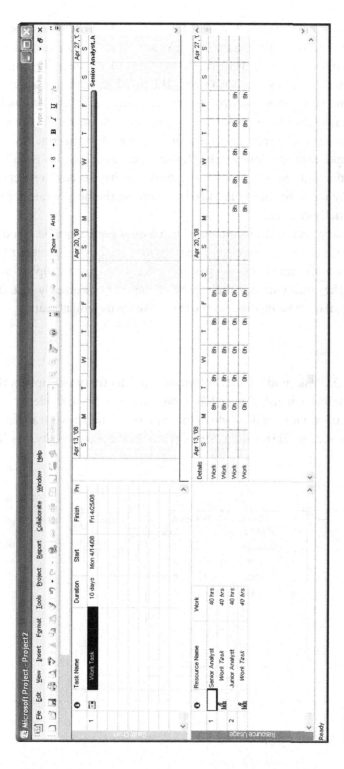

FIGURE 1.25
Manually enter hours for each resource.

could guess at how many additional hours are needed for the task and add that in. Or, the project planner can specify that the junior analyst is working 100% of his or her time on the task and then reduce the number of hours that the junior analyst works. The problem with this approach is that, if the task shifts, the work hours no longer reflect the productivity loss because they were entered for a specific date. The results are even more erroneous if the resource is not fully allocated to this one task but instead is split among several tasks. Those other tasks are also penalized from a productivity perspective. Lastly, to ensure that the costs reflect this productivity loss, the user is required to increase the hourly rate for the lower productivity days.

In summary, using Microsoft Project to assess even a simple resource shift on a project is an exercise in *gaming the system*. The project manager spends more time tweaking parameter values to get an approximate picture of the situation, and the reality of the event is quickly lost. Try explaining all of these changes to the executive management team.

pmBLOX

The pmBLOX task model includes dynamic productivity multipliers that are available for each task. Figure 1.26 shows how easy it is to model a rather complex situation for a task in which the resource ownership is transferred to a less knowledgeable resource. Simply enter in the productivity loss. The

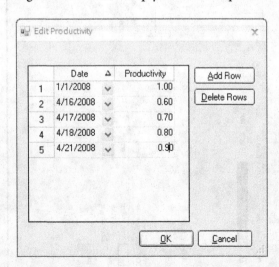

FIGURE 1.26
pmBLOX productivity multiplier.

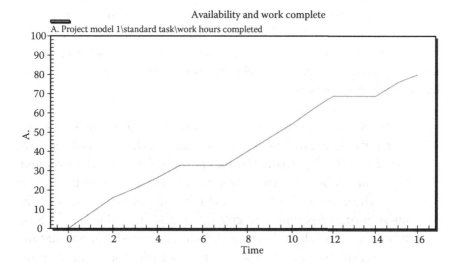

FIGURE 1.27
Increased task duration as a result of a resource shift.

user can even enter in an expected ramp up in the resource's knowledge of the task.

This example shows a resource shift occurring on April 16. The new resource quickly ramps up over the next four days but never quite reaches the level of productivity of the original resource that is assigned to the task (i.e., only 90%, not the full 100%). The results from the simulation are shown in Figure 1.27. The task takes 16 days, as would occur in the real world, and not the optimistic 10 days that is seen in Microsoft Project.

WHAT DOES THIS MEAN FOR PROJECT MANAGERS?

The three issues and the two test cases point out significant misleading algorithms that are used in Microsoft Project. For project managers, this means that these types of misleading results are compounded for larger and more complex projects. If these types of misleading results can be seen on a few simple tasks, imagine how many times these misleading results occur when there are more tasks that are more complicated in their dependencies? Going back to the earlier discussion of Table 1.1, it is now easy to see how larger projects produce bigger errors. Simply put, there are more opportunities for Microsoft Project (or any other CPM-based tool) to apply these misleading algorithms. The more opportunities there are, the more the final results differ from realistic and accurate results.

In summary, the resulting problems are the following (each problem in the list builds on the previous problem, culminating with the worst problem at the bottom of the list):

- *Assumptions are not adequately challenged.* Most people assume that any software tool can provide the most realistic and correct calculations. That is usually the sole purpose for using the software; it provides a better answer than we humans can calculate on our own. Thus, the output from many of these software tools is rarely questioned and is simply accepted. For large and complex projects, it becomes difficult to challenge the underlying assumptions that are used to drive the project inputs. Assumptions are not captured in any meaningful way due to the focus on duration, so it quickly becomes a *shell game* of changing durations to *fit* what we expect to happen. For example, it is not uncommon for a project manager to be given the defined starting date for a project and the expected completion date for the project, and the project manager's job is to draw a Gantt chart that fits within those dates, regardless of the plausibility of the plan.

- *Project plans are difficult to defend.* Because assumptions are not explicitly captured, and the calculations by Microsoft Project (or any other CPM-based tool) are often misleading, output results are difficult to defend because there is typically very little justification. Why is this task only 10 days long? Because that is what the software tells us it is. Can all this work be completed even with overallocated resources? Yes, because that is what the software tells us. When a project manager is asked for details on a particular task, all that can be provided as a defense are the number of allocated resources, the expected work level of these resources, and the duration of the task. These inputs may be completely unrealistic, but the tools provide no mechanism for capturing any other information about the task, so defending this small set of inputs in any meaningful way becomes difficult.

- *Cost and schedule risks increase.* As stated several times in this chapter, the simple methods of current tools provide misleading results. There are two major consequences of this that increase the cost and schedule risks for the project. First, expectations are set to unrealistic levels. Can the project be done in 10 months? Sure, that is what the tool tells us, so let us share that with everyone. Now, everyone in the organization expects this to happen. Furthermore, all the resources are committed, along with shipment schedules to suppliers, deliveries to customers, etc. Everything is synchronized to this misleading schedule. When the project does not progress according to this plan (which is very common due to the misleading output), all these synchronized connections need to be shifted and recoordinated. Second, when things change in a project, as they often do, the tools are insufficient for replanning and rescheduling the project to an achievable end. In essence, the issues already mentioned are compounded through the replanning and rescheduling process. The new plan and schedule are just as misleading as the original baseline plan and schedule. It is the illusion of control.

- *The probability of project success decreases.* The ultimate result of these problems is that the probability of success for the project (i.e., the probability that the project will meet its cost and schedule estimates) decreases significantly. The projects require superhuman effort to get back on track to be successful because they have started in a terrible state with regards to what is truly possible. They start *from behind* and must expend enormous effort to even *catch up* to what the plan states should happen. When these projects fail, and the team conducts a post mortem to capture the lessons that are learned, these observations point to activities like better coordination, better visibility of project progress, etc. Until the tools change to incorporate more realistic parameters and methods, there will always be coordination and visibility issues. There are wonderful and capable project managers out there, but they are at a severe disadvantage using woefully insufficient planning and management tools. The cycle continues.

In a nutshell, the project planning and management tools currently available, like Microsoft Project, allow project managers to create completely unrealistic and unachievable plans. The tools do not offer enough checkpoints because this information is not needed for the simplistic models and methods that are used by the tools. In the current fast-paced, ever-changing business world, simple methods are no longer sufficient. In fact, they are dangerous. They create the biggest risk that any project can experience: an unrealistic baseline plan. Right from the start, the project manager and project team are fighting an uphill battle.

The graphic in Figure 1.28 does a good job of capturing the recent difficulties that are faced by current project managers. Metaphorically, we

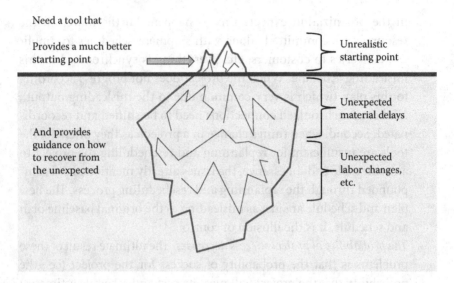

Need a tool that

Provides a much better starting point

And provides guidance on how to recover from the unexpected

Unrealistic starting point

Unexpected material delays

Unexpected labor changes, etc.

FIGURE 1.28
Just the tip of the iceberg.

have just discussed the text on the left side of the *tip of the iceberg*, which indicates that the current project managers need a tool that provides a much better starting point (i.e., baseline plan). In the text on the right side of the graphic, without a realistic starting point (i.e., starting with an unrealistic baseline plan), the project manager and project team have difficulty getting back on track when unexpected material delays, labor changes, etc., occur during the course of the project because the current project planning and management tools, like Microsoft Project, do a very poor job of accommodating these types of real-world issues into their simple models and methods. Following the text on the left side of the graphic, a tool like pmBLOX using the DPM not only provides a better starting point with a more realistic baseline plan but also enables project managers and project teams to better understand what options are available to them for recovering from unexpected delays. More of the details of the DPM will be discussed in later chapters and will shed light on how this is accomplished.

REFERENCE

Brooks, Jr., F. P. 1975. *The Mythical Man-Month: Essays on Software Engineering*. Boston: Addison-Wesley Publishing Company. (ISBN 0-201-00650-2).

2

Why "Dynamic Progress Method?"

INTRODUCTION

Along the way through this Defense Advanced Research Project Agency (DARPA) research, the authors have been asked several times about the name Dynamic Progress Method (DPM) and its official definition. The motivation for the name comes from the definitions of the first two words, according to Merriam-Webster (http://www.merriam-webster.com):

- Dynamic—always active or changing
- Progress—movement forward or toward a place

These two words capture the essence of the project planning and management problem. As the project manager and project team try to move the project forward toward its goal(s), things are always changing along the way. Nothing is static, and nothing is straightforward and simple. Corrections are constantly needed to keep the project heading in the right direction. If the basic information used to ascertain the status of the project is flawed, it becomes extremely difficult to know which corrections to make (and when to make them) to get the project back on course (i.e., back on schedule or back on budget). Suppose that an airplane had a navigation system with poor accuracy that was 1 mi. off of the true position of the airplane (randomly in any direction). Imagine trying to guide this airplane to its destination, and, more importantly, visualize attempting to land it. Or, if flying is not a good analogy for the readers, imagine driving a car that had a speedometer with poor accuracy that was 10 or 20 mi./h off of the true speed of the car (randomly above or below). It would be very difficult to drive the correct speed on the highway. In essence, if the baseline plan is incorrect or flawed, it is difficult to manage according to this baseline or any revision of this baseline. The biggest risk for any project is to start with a poor baseline estimate. The project manager and project team are doomed from the beginning and are always playing catch-up.

The basis of the DPM is the consideration of a system and, specifically, treating a project as a business system. The following sections walk through the thought process that brought the authors to the research hypothesis that the planning tools used by project managers are too simplistic to provide reasonable estimates for cost and schedule, which leads to many project difficulties.

UNDERSTANDING SYSTEMS AND SYSTEM COMPLEXITY

There are several definitions for a system, but the most generic and practical is that a system is a group of parts or components that work together to achieve a common goal or objective. For example, every person has many body parts that combine to form the human body and its systems, which have goals such as growth and survival. In a business organization, employees and groups work together to achieve the organization's goals, such as higher market share and technological leadership.

We can define a system's main elements as the parts (or entities, components, etc.) that perform the work and the relations (or interconnections, interactions, etc.) that define how the parts combine together and how the work of the system will be accomplished. Obviously, both parts and relations are important for a system to perform adequately. For instance, looking at the human body again as an example, each part of the body must know how to connect and coordinate with the other parts. The brain has to signal the mouth to chew food, which gets swallowed and digested to provide energy for the body to move and conduct activities. Some of these relations are voluntary and actively controlled by us (e.g., picking up food, chewing, swallowing), and some of these are involuntary (e.g., heartbeat, digestion, release of enzymes). The same concept can be applied to business systems in organizations. A business system, or process, must have skilled employees working together in an effective manner. The employees, information technology systems, facilities, etc., represent the parts of the business system, and the procedures, processes, coordination, and communication among them represent the relations.

If the quantity of parts in a system is graphed against the quantity of relations, as in Figure 2.1, we can begin to define the complexity of the system. Systems that have few parts and few relations among those parts can be considered simple systems or systems with low complexity. On the other end of the spectrum, systems with many parts and many relations among those parts can be considered complex systems or systems with high complexity.

Consider a sports analogy. A golf team can be considered a simple system. The authors are not saying that golf is simple. It requires great skills, but from a system perspective, a team of golfers can be considered a simple system. With a golf team, the score of the team is the sum of the scores of the individual players. However, the individual players cannot directly affect the performance of other individuals on the team. Other than some motivational pep talks and encouragement, any one player does not have a direct impact on any other player's performance. If treated like a system, the team has few parts (i.e., only four individual players), and there are very few relations among those parts, which makes it a simple system.

On the other hand, consider a soccer or football team. There are many more players (up to 11) that act as the parts of the system. The relations are the way the players work together (i.e., their *teamwork*). Both the players and teamwork are important to the team's success. If each of the players does not understand the fundamentals of the game, such as dribbling and passing the ball for soccer and blocking and tackling for football, the team will not do well, regardless of how well the players work together.

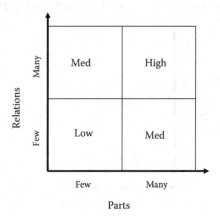

FIGURE 2.1
System complexity grid.

Moreover, the team will still be unsuccessful if all the players have excellent individual skills yet refuse to pass the ball (in soccer) or coordinate with other players (running plays in football). Just as with golf, the score of the team is the sum of the scores of the individual players on the team. However, in this regard, it is possible for one player to directly impact another player's performance. If one player never passes the soccer ball to a teammate, that teammate cannot score regardless of how good he or she is. In football, if the quarterback never hands off the ball to the running back, that running back cannot score a touchdown regardless of how good he or she is. As a result, it is very possible for a team of mediocre players to defeat a team of superstars because the former have better teamwork. This phenomenon has been seen often in the sports world when an underdog team with less skillful players defeats a team of very skillful players. If treated like a system, the soccer or football team has many parts (i.e., 11 individual players), and there are many relations among those parts (i.e., coordinating on plays), which makes it a complex system (Figure 2.2).

When a business process is not achieving the desired results, the traditional response is to encourage employees to work harder and better. Or, continuing with the sports analogy, the typical response is to encourage the players to try harder and put more effort into the game. This represents a focus on the system's parts. The belief is that if each individual part performs better, the entire system will perform better.

In the business world, slogans and posters such as "Do your best!" and "We're counting on you to make a difference!" point to the individual employees as the reason why a process is performing poorly or yielding

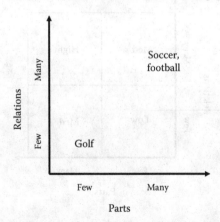

FIGURE 2.2
Sports as examples of simple and complex systems.

poor results (Pryor et al. 1998, 2007). As many readers can testify, this is a very frustrating situation to be caught in. Usually, the process is broken because of the ineffective manner in which the employees are forced to coordinate. Most employees are very limited in their power to make changes to a process or organization.

A better and more effective response to inefficient processes is to focus on the system's relations. Alter the workflow, eliminate activities, collocate personnel, or make similar changes. The recent field of systems thinking emphasizes this point strongly. One of the first systems thinkers, Jay Forrester, states in his groundbreaking 1961 book, *Industrial Dynamics* (Forrester, 1961), that we can expect that the interconnections, interactions, and relationships among the components of the system will typically be more important than each of the components in isolation by themselves. In *The Fifth Discipline* (1990), author Peter Senge builds upon this idea by stating that the leverage for change or improvement of a system is found in the structure, or relations, of the system. In systems thinking, relations themselves tend to take on their own identity. The term synergy applies here. Synergy occurs at the level of relations in a system. The phrase "the total is greater than the sum of the parts" points to this concept.

Looking at the system complexity grid from Figure 2.1, we can establish a model for focusing efforts to improve a system. In a complex system, relations dominate and have a substantial effect on the system's success. At the opposite extreme, in a simple system, the system's individual parts dominate and primarily determine the system's success. This is shown in Figure 2.3.

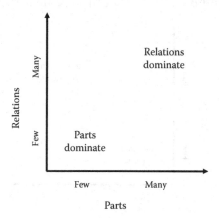

FIGURE 2.3
Parts dominate performance in simple systems, and relations dominate performance in complex systems.

To improve a football or soccer team or any other type of complex system in which the relations dominate, the focus must be primarily on the relations since the relations primarily determine the level of performance of the system. As stated in the preceding paragraphs in this same section, the parts do impact system performance, and the parts of the system (e.g., the players) need to have the necessary skill sets. But, to dramatically improve the performance of the complex system, the relations must be changed. Conversely, to improve a golf team or any type of simple system in which the individual parts dominate, the focus must be primarily on the individual parts since they tend to operate in isolation with a high degree of independence. This is shown in Figure 2.4.

For business systems, we can extend this model to incorporate business process reengineering and continuous process improvement. For instance, consider the traditional engineering company that is organized by functions. It can be considered a complex system because it has many parts that interact with many relations to meet its objective. However, it is often treated and managed like a simple system in which the individual parts do not interact significantly. Generally, work flows from design to planning to manufacturing. An individual within each functional area does his or her portion of the work and throws the work *over the wall* to the next step in the process. Now, suppose that this process is producing unsatisfactory results. If the company was simply to improve each functional area separately, this improvement effort would represent focusing on the parts of the system (as if it were a simple system). The positive results would be minimal. In fact, in this example, the results are often

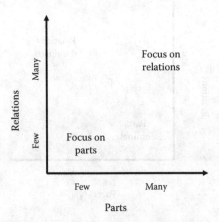

FIGURE 2.4
Where to focus to improve the system performance.

worse. As each functional area attempts to optimize its portion of the process, the total process becomes suboptimized and more confusing to those who are participating. However, as an example, if the company improved the process by collocating personnel from each of the separate functional areas and changing the reward program to a team-based incentive, this improvement effort would represent a focus on the relations of the system and would produce better results. Enhanced communication and team appraisals would represent new relationships among team members.

In this example, as in many process improvements, the major problems in business systems and processes are not with the individual employees. The employees are simply acting in accordance with the system that they are in. If they do not communicate often, it is because they are isolated and working with different standards or not encouraged or incentivized to communicate. In addition, the reward program may encourage individual effort as opposed to team success. The real problem lies in the system structure of separating employees who need to share critical and timely information. Change this structure, and the process will generate new results.

The concepts in Figures 2.3 and 2.4 are summarized in the following bulleted lists for business systems (processes).

Focus on individual parts (i.e., employees and small work groups) of a system or process when

- Minimal improvements are desired.
- Relations cannot be changed.
- The system is simple and does not have many relations (i.e., high degree of independence).

Examples of how to focus on parts are the following:

- Educate employees about the process of which they are a part.
- Train the employees in the necessary skills for their activities.
- Show employees their spans of control.
- Ensure that all employees are receiving necessary resources.

Focus on the relations (i.e., procedures, coordination, and communication) of a system or process when

- Major improvements are desired.
- Improvement of individual parts has yielded minimal results.
- The system is complex and dominated by relations.

The examples of how to focus on relations are the following:

- Reevaluate process objectives.
- Eliminate as much handling of the product as possible.
- Eliminate buffer inventories between activities.
- Establish teams that include all necessary disciplines and cross-train members.
- Flowchart the process with participation from all team members.

In summary, any process or system (such as a large project) is composed of individual parts that perform the work of the system and relations that describe how the work should be accomplished. In complex systems that contain many parts and relations (such as large projects), the relations typically determine the system's performance. Therefore, understanding these relations and including them in any type of project planning or analysis effort are paramount.

CLASSES OF BUSINESS MODELS

To begin to understand how the current, duration-based critical path method (CPM) approach is detrimental to project planning and management, it is useful to first look at the different classes of business models. As shown in Figure 2.5, there are three major classes of business models: (1) ad hoc, (2) analytical, and (3) operational. These classes range in fidelity from low to high, indicated by the arrow on the left side of the diagram.

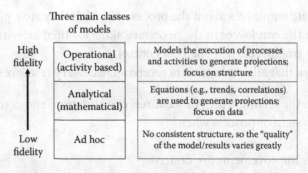

FIGURE 2.5
Modeling business systems.

A definition of fidelity is "the degree to which something matches or copies something else" (http://www.merriam-webster.com). Thus, for the purposes of this discussion, fidelity refers to how realistically the class of model captures the elements that are found in the real-world system where this is being modeled.

Ad hoc models have no consistency or standardization. The capabilities of these models are strongly dependent on the skills of the model developer. As such, there is a great deal of variation among ad hoc models of the same system. Each developer may choose different elements of the system to focus on, or the connections between two parts of the system may be represented in very different ways among multiple developers. As a result, ad hoc models are considered to have the lowest level of fidelity or realism.

Analytical models, also called mathematical models, are models for which there is a solution that can be directly calculated. This means that a user can input various parameters and calculate at the same time for all the variables in the system for all periods of time. For example, the determination of the future value (FV) of a current or present value (PV) of money is an analytical model

$$FV = PV \times (1 + i)^t,$$

where i is the interest rate, and t represents the time period in years.

With the FV equation, the value for time period 1 can be directly calculated (by setting $t = 1$), and the value for time period 10 can be directly calculated (by setting $t = 10$). For example, consider the simple example in which the PV is $1000 and the interest rate (i) is 10%. The FV equation becomes

$$FV = \$1000 \times (1.10)^t.$$

If we want to calculate the FV in one year, we set $t = 1$, and the answer is the following:

$$FV = \$1000 \times (1.10) = \$1100.$$

If we want to calculate the FV in 10 years, we set $t = 10$, and the answer is the following:

$$FV = \$1000 \times (1.10)^{10} = \$2593.74.$$

Of course, this is a very simple analytical model. Those used in businesses, such as a sales forecasting models or an inventory-to-sales correlation models, are much more complex and involve many more variables, which is why analytical models are considered a level higher in fidelity than ad hoc models (which may contain only a few relevant variables based on the limited knowledge of the model developer). But, the concept is the same. Each variable of concern can be directly calculated for all time periods. Consequently, analytical models draw heavily from historical or other data. Data are the foundation. Without data, the analytical models used for business systems are severely curtailed.

Operational models capture the *operations* or *activities* that occur in a system and attempt to mimic them in the same manner as they occur. As a result, operational models tend to include the interconnections and relations among the various parts of the system. Operational models are used when the system of concern is so complex or complicated that simple direct calculations of the FVs of variables are not possible. In this case, we simulate when we cannot calculate. The operational model treats each time period separately, and the only way for the model to know what happens in the tenth time period is to know what happens in the first time period, then the second time period (based on the results of the first time period), then the third time period (based on the results of the second time period), and so on. Because of this type of approach, operational models have the highest level of fidelity or realism.

Note: Any analytical model can be translated into an operational model, but typically an operational model cannot be translated into an analytical model without simplifying or removing many of the interconnections of the various variables (which is the key purpose of the operational model).

If operational models have the highest level of fidelity, then why are operational models not used all the time? There are several reasons why they are not:

- *Operational model development is a difficult skill set.* Not all people can build operational models, and those who do have typically taken advanced courses and spent a great deal of time to develop and hone the skill.
- *Operational model development often takes longer than analytical or ad hoc model development because of all the model details that must be included.* In many cases, we do not have the luxury of spending large chunks of time to develop operational models.

- *Depending on the system or the portion of the system being modeled, operational models may require details that are not relevant to the problem at hand, such as a very aggregate view of a situation.* In these cases, analytical or ad hoc models may suffice.

Considering the bulleted comments above, in any modeling effort for a business system, the class or *complexity* of the model (and, therefore, the level of fidelity of the model and the time and resources it take to develop the model) should match the complexity of the system (Figure 2.6). Larger and more complex business systems require a more realistic (high-fidelity) modeling approach to capture sufficient detail, which reduces risk. This is called *balancing risk and reality.* It is not economical to use complex (i.e., high-fidelity) modeling approaches for simple systems or processes. The risk here is that the model development takes a nonproportional amount of time and resources compared to the gain that will be received from the modeling effort. A common saying for this is, "The juice is not worth the squeeze." The cost of the development outweighs the benefits of the development. Conversely, it is too risky to use simple (i.e., low-fidelity) modeling approaches on complex systems or processes because there is value in understanding the details of the complex system. Relations and interconnections dominate the performance of the complex system. Thus, if these relations and interconnections are not included or simplified or *assumed away,* there is a high risk that the model results will provide misleading or absolutely incorrect answers.

While the concept of balancing the modeling approach to the level of system complexity is valid, more details of the modeling approaches need

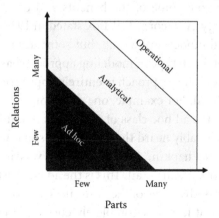

FIGURE 2.6
Matching model classes to system complexity.

General description

			General description
High fidelity	Operational (activity based)	System dynamics simulation	Focuses on structure of *system* and not data; incorporates feedback and relationships among variables
		Discrete event simulation	Captures operations of each activity; links activities to understand overall performance; requires detailed data
	Analytical (mathematical)	Network model	Models tasks as network nodes; various methods for how work flows through nodes; critical path method; PERT
		Parametric model	Makes projections by fitting curves to historical data; relies heavily on lots of *clean* data for accurate curve
	Ad hoc	Spreadsheet	Adds some structure to estimation; build-up approach; matches resources against tasks; most common approach
Low fidelity		Best guess	Projections based on analogous efforts; unstructured; relies on instinct or *gut feeling*; pencil and paper

FIGURE 2.7
Modeling technologies.

to be introduced to be able to make this happen. Figure 2.7 breaks out the three classes of models into more specific modeling approaches that fall within these classes. This is not a complete list. However, it contains the major modeling approaches within each class and is sufficient for the discussion in this book that is related to the CPM, the DPM, and treating projects as systems. In Figure 2.7, the three classes are broken down into six modeling technologies ranging from lowest fidelity to highest fidelity: (1) best guess, (2) spreadsheet, (3) parametric model, (4) network model, (5) discrete event simulation, and (6) system dynamics simulation. For each modeling technology, a short description is provided.

Figure 2.8 points out some of the benefits and disadvantages of each modeling technology. As George E.P. Box stated in 1987 (Box and Draper, 1987, p. 424), "…all models are wrong, but some are useful." Essentially, no model is perfect. Each type of modeling approach has its strengths and weaknesses. No modeling approach is entirely appropriate for all types of systems to be modeled. For example, one of the main benefits of the best-guess approach (in the ad hoc class of models) is that it is quick and easy. The readers have probably heard the phrase that something was drawn or done on the "back of a napkin," indicating that it was done in haste, in the moment, and without much detail. This is the ad hoc best-guess approach. To counter this, a disadvantage of the best-guess approach is that it is typically not correct or at least not completely correct. Simplifying assumptions had to be made along the way. As a result, the best-guess approach is difficult to defend because it is often just based on someone's *gut feeling*,

			Benefits	Disadvantages
High fidelity	Operational (activity based)	System dynamics simulation	Captures feedback loops; relates cause to effect	Aggregate approach; not for detailed problems
		Discrete event simulation	Captures details of activities; relates cause to effect	Lacks feedback among variables
	Analytical (mathematical)	Network model	Excellent for understanding relations among activities	Cumbersome when used for high-level problems
		Parametric model	Well accepted; many tools available	Data dependent; assumes future will be same as past
Low fidelity	Ad hoc	Spreadsheet	Little training required; easy to understand	Applies to unique problem; dependent on model builder
		Best guess	Easiest and quickest to use	Typically inaccurate; often difficult to defend

FIGURE 2.8
Benefits and disadvantages of modeling technologies.

which may or may not have any true bearing on the situation. Within the ad hoc class of models, the only real tool is the spreadsheet.

At the other end of the spectrum, consider the system dynamics method of simulation (in the operational class of models). One of the primary strengths of system dynamics is that it can incorporate connections among variables, which end up driving feedback loops within the system. A feedback loop is where an action takes place, and the information that results from that action is used to determine if or how much of that action should continue. A simple example is pouring a glass of water. One would pour quickly when the glass is empty, but the rate of pouring would slow down (feedback) as the glass fills up with water until eventually the rate of pouring would stop when the glass is full (assuming that we are trying not to spill the water). In this example, the feedback is provided by our eyes as we watch the glass fill with water. An example of a feedback loop in a company is the budgeting cycle that a company may use. Every month or quarter (or whatever the desired period of time), the executives of a company may get together to check the status of current spending against the proposed annual budget. If the spending is higher than the budget, there is an attempt to cut costs (i.e., slow down spending much like we slowed down the rate of pouring into our glass) to bring spending back in line with the approved budget. A weakness of system dynamics, up to this point, is that it is typically only appropriate for aggregate models. So, the system that is being modeled would have to be a high-level, aggregate system and not a very detailed system. (This concept will be discussed more in Chapter 5 with the comparison of typical system dynamics models of projects with the DPM.)

Figure 2.9 summarizes the concept of the table in Figure 2.8 by laying out the two ends of the modeling technology spectrum across the system complexity grid. Recalling Figure 2.6, which matches model complexity and fidelity with system complexity, a spreadsheet would be most appropriate for simple systems (or processes or projects). A spreadsheet would not be appropriate for modeling complex systems (or processes or projects) because it cannot capture the key relationships and feedback loops that exist in and drive performance in the complex system. Thus, there would not be a balance of risk and reality. Instead, we would have to accept the risk that the low-fidelity approach of the spreadsheet would result in oversimplification of the complex system. The model would not be very realistic at all.

For complex systems (or processes or projects), system dynamics simulation is the most appropriate. The system dynamics simulation model could capture all the key relationships and feedback loops that exist in and drive performance in the complex system. Risk and reality would be balanced. It would be worth the time and effort to develop the system dynamics model because the benefits of simulating the detailed inner workings of the complex system would provide information on how to improve the performance of the system. Yet, a system dynamics model is overkill for a simple system that has very few relations and feedback loops among the isolated and independent parts of the system. The strength of the system dynamics approach (feedback loops) would not be put to use.

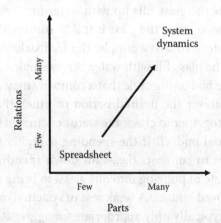

FIGURE 2.9

Mapping modeling technologies to system complexity.

Thus, after expending a lot of time and energy to develop a system dynamics model of a simple system, the results would not provide much performance improvement.

SYSTEM COMPLEXITY AND PROJECT COMPLEXITY

This discussion up to this point in this chapter has covered the concept of a system and how it relates to businesses. As stated earlier in the "Introduction" section in this chapter, the basis of the DPM is that we can treat a project within an organization as a system. Thus, we needed to learn more about the makeup and nature of business systems, which can range from simple to complex. More specifically, if a project can be considered a business system, then projects can range from simple (i.e., few resources used with very little interaction among the resources) to complex (i.e., many resources used with a great deal of interaction and dependency among the resources). Keeping with the concept that risk and reality need to be balanced, the current CPM and the new DPM can now be charted on the system complexity grid (Figure 2.10). The CPM is sufficient for simple projects, but it quickly becomes woefully insufficient for capturing the details of large and complex projects. The DPM is appropriate for complex projects. Although it could be used for simple projects, it may prove to be overkill and require more time and effort than is necessary.

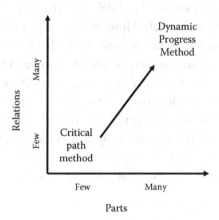

FIGURE 2.10
CPM compared to DPM with system complexity.

Commercially available tools

High fidelity	Operational (activity based)	System dynamics simulation	pmBLOX
		Discrete event simulation	ProjectSimulator
	Analytical (mathematical)	Network model	Primavera, ProChain, PERTMaster
		Parametric model	PRICE, SEER, CoCoMo
	Ad hoc	Spreadsheet	Microsoft project
Low fidelity		Best guess	

FIGURE 2.11
Project management tools using various modeling technologies.

Figure 2.11 provides the readers with a mapping of currently available project management tools to the classes of models (and, thus, to the complexity of the project). As they will see, Microsoft Project, which uses the CPM, is essentially a massive spreadsheet database that provides a static (nonchanging) view of a project. As such, it is appropriate for simple projects that are short in duration, do not use many resources, and do not involve a great deal of interaction and dependencies among the resources and project tasks. Other tools fill in the analytical class of models. At the operational class level (with high fidelity), there are only two available tools: (1) ProjectSimulator (discrete event simulation) and (2) pmBLOX® (system dynamics simulation). As shown in Figure 2.7, the system dynamics method has the highest level of fidelity (realism), so it becomes appropriate for very complex projects. However, remember from Figure 2.8 that a weakness of the system dynamics method is that it tends to be used only for aggregate representations. Yet, to realistically model a complex project, the modeling approach must be able to go down to the level of granularity of a single task and a single resource completing work for that task. With the DPM and the resulting tool pmBLOX, this has been accomplished, so this weakness no longer exists for project models. This will be discussed further in Chapters 5 and 6.

When simple tools are used for complex projects, many issues are created:

- Assumptions are not challenged, and there is no strong basis for challenging them.

- All resources are considered equal. However, they are not, and simply changing the resources for a project (without changing the dependencies among the tasks) can have detrimental impacts.
- Resource leveling within the tool is often inconsistent, or worse, it is sometimes not even possible, so the project manager is left to figure it out for himself or herself.
- The project plan is static and does not account for changes that may occur along the course of the project.
- The project plan is often difficult to defend due to the lack of straight-forward logic.
- Cost and schedule risks increase.
- The probability of project success decreases significantly.

INTRODUCING THE DPM

The purpose of this chapter is to discuss the reasons for calling this approach the Dynamic Progress Method. From the earlier sections, the readers can see the line of thought and reasoning that brought the authors to the hypothesis of their research effort for DARPA, which is essentially that the current project planning tools are based on simplistic methods that do not capture the realism that is necessary for complex projects. Hence, the cost and schedule estimates provided by these simple planning tools are misleading and at times incorrect, which contributes to the low success rate of current projects. The proposed solution by the authors is to create an operational simulation of the allocation of resources to accomplish project work, which can provide more realistic, achievable, and defendable estimates for cost and schedule.

The official definition of the DPM is as follows:

The Dynamic Progress Method is an approach for estimating the cost and schedule of a project by operationally simulating the allocation of resources on each project task to accomplish a backlog of work for each task, as well as the various management actions that might be taken to change the allocation of resources and the productivity impacts of these changes on the resources.

It is the operational simulation of the allocation of resources and the accomplishment of work that sets the DPM apart from the program evaluation and review technique/CPM and provides the foundation for realism, as highlighted in Figure 2.10. In fact, from this point, there can be four levels of realism that are possible within the DPM, each building on the previous level:

1. *Level 1*: Operational simulation of resource allocation and work accomplishment
2. *Level 2*: Resource productivity
3. *Level 3*: Management actions
4. *Level 4*: Productivity impacts of management actions

All of these will be discussed in more detail in Chapters 5 and 6 with the more specific descriptions of the underlying DPM simulation model.

REFERENCES

Box, G. E. P. and N. R. Draper. 1987. *Empirical Model-Building and Response Surfaces.* Hoboken, NJ: Wiley (ISBN-10: 0471810339).
Forrester, J. W. 1961. *Industrial Dynamics.* Portland, OR: Productivity Press.
Pryor, M. G., J. C. White, and L. Toombs. 1998, 2007. *Strategic Quality Management: A Strategic Systems Approach to Continuous Improvement.* Mason, OH: Thompson Learning, republished by Boston: Cengage Learning (ISBN-10: 0873934164, ISBN-13: 978-0873934169).
Senge, P. M. 1990. *The Fifth Discipline: The Art & Practice of the Learning Organization.* New York: Doubleday/Currency.
White, J. C. 1995. The Bermuda Triangle of traditional business assumptions. *Industrial Management,* 37(5). Norcross, GA: Institute of Industrial Engineers (IIE). Sep/Oct.
White, J. C. 1996. Reengineering and continuous improvement. *Quality Digest,* July. Available at http://www.qualitydigest.com/jul/contimp.html (accessed February 6, 2015).

3

The Current Status
of Project Management

You may con a person into committing to an unreasonable deadline, but
you cannot bully them into meeting it.

Edwards, Butler, Hill, and Russell

The biggest risk for any project is an unrealistic baseline plan.

J. Chris White

INTRODUCTION

A great deal of research has been done on the current status of project
management, especially the amount of project *failures* and the possible
underlying reasons for why they occur. Failure is purposely italicized
because the definition of a project failure differs among many of the
reports, as well as the actual findings. The reference list at the end of this
chapter provides the readers with a starting point for research, reports,
and findings to learn more.

From all the research, the authors cannot pinpoint exactly how many
project failures there are and the exact reasons for why they occur.
However, a few broad points can definitely be made that all of the current
and past research and reports can validate.

PROJECT FAILURE RATES ARE GREATER THAN ZERO

First, it is unanimously agreed that the rate of project failures is greater than 0%. Or, to put that another way, the amount of project successes is less than 100%. In other words, some or perhaps many projects indeed fail. All research supports this, with the rate of failure falling somewhere between 1% and 99%. That may sound like a silly statement, but let us just look at two major reports to see the differences:

1. The Standish Group is well known for its CHAOS reports that have analyzed project success and failure rates for information technology (IT) projects. The project resolution results from the 2012 CHAOS research indicate the following:
   - About 39% of projects succeeded (i.e., delivered on time, on budget, with required features and functions).
   - About 43% of projects were challenged (i.e., late and/or over budget and/or with less than the required features).
   - About 18% of projects failed (i.e., cancelled prior to completion or delivered and never used).

   Looking at the data slightly differently, the report states that, on average, only 69% of originally proposed features have been provided on these projects. Cost overruns have been on the order of 59%, on average, and schedule overruns have been on the order of 74%, on average. Compare these numbers to the results of the Defense Advanced Research Project Agency (DARPA) research by the authors that were presented in Chapter 1. In the DARPA research project, cost overruns were on the order of 26%, and schedule overruns were on the order of 54%.

2. The Project Management Institute (PMI) is the premier project management organization in the world and is well respected for its research and analysis of the project management industry. According to the Pulse of the Profession report published by the PMI in 2015, the percentage of projects that meet the objectives has remained steady at 64% for several years. This means that about one-third of projects fail to meet their intended objectives. Compare this 64% success rate to the 39% success rate that is suggested by the 2012 CHAOS report. They are almost the converse of each other. One report suggests that two out of three projects are successful, and only one out of three

projects does not succeed, whereas another report suggests that only one out of three projects is successful, and two out of three projects do not succeed.

Both of these reports are valid and based on solid research methods, yet they show significantly different results. Suffice it to say that a good amount of projects today are unsuccessful.

Why do we care that the rate of project failures is greater than 0%? It means that the project management industry still has work to do. Can we expect perfection all the time? No, but all research agrees and validates that changes can be incorporated that would decrease the rate of project failures. Any project failure is a waste of time and resources, and every organization, whether for profit or not for profit, should care that time, money, and other resources are being wasted. If the organization is for profit, this directly translates to bottom-line profit increases. If the company can do the same work and accomplish the same objectives with less time, less money, and less effort, the company directly and quickly benefits. If the organization is not for profit, this directly translates to a greater capacity to provide the organization's benefit or service to a larger group of people or a larger geographical area. It improves the stewardship of limited and scarce resources.

LARGER PROJECTS SUFFER MORE THAN SMALLER PROJECTS

Second, it is unanimously agreed that the rate of project failures for large projects is greater than the rate of project failures for small projects. This matches the results that the authors saw on the DARPA research project that was described in Chapter 1. Furthermore, it matches the results from the 2012 CHAOS report. Table 3.1 shows the breakout of the overall success rate of projects into small projects (less than $1 million in labor content) and large projects (over $10 million in labor content). Notice that only 10% of large projects succeed, based on the CHAOS research.

One of the main reasons why project failures occur at a proportional rate compared to the size of the project (i.e., small projects have small rates of failure, medium projects have medium rates of failure, and large projects have large rates of failure) is simply that there are more opportunities

TABLE 3.1

2012 CHAOS Results on Project Success Rates

	Small Projects	Large Projects	Overall
Successful	76%	10%	39%
Challenged	20%	52%	43%
Failed	4%	38%	18%

for failure. Consider Metcalfe's law (named after Robert Metcalfe), which characterizes many of the network effects of communication technologies and things like the Internet and social networking. Metcalfe's law has often been used to express the value of a node in a network, such as a connection in a social network. One person alone has no connections and, therefore, no value (in this example with regards to the social network). But, the value of each additional person into the social network increases the value to all the people in the network because the total number of connections to and from any one person greatly increase. And, the greater the number of people in the social network, the greater its value. Mathematically, the number of unique connections in a network of *nodes* (e.g., people, computers, parts in a system, tasks in a project) are governed by the following equation:

$$\text{Number of connections} = N \times (N - 1)/2.$$

Figure 3.1 shows this graphically for a set of three nodes ($N = 3$) and four nodes ($N = 4$). The number of connections or relations with three nodes is three, while the number of connections or relations with four nodes is six:

$$\text{Number of connections}(3) = 3 \times (3-1)/2$$
$$= 6/2$$
$$N = 3$$
$$\text{Number of connections}(4) = 4 \times (4-1)/2$$
$$= 12/2$$
$$= 6$$
$$N = 4$$

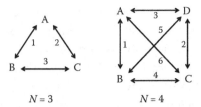

FIGURE 3.1
Example of Metcalfe's law.

Figure 3.2 takes the math a little bit further to show the shape of the curve that is generated by this equation, which is exponential. That means that the marginal value of each additional node (or part) added to the system is greater than the marginal value of the previous node that was added to the system. As can be seen in the table, the number of relations for three parts is 3, and the number of relations for four parts is 6, which is an increase of three relations; the number of relations for five parts is 10, which is an increase of four relations; the number of relations for six parts is 15, which is an increase of five relations; and so on. The additional relations with each part get larger and larger.

All this math basically means that there are more opportunities for mistakes because there are more *moving parts* in the system. The following analogy is not perfectly correct, but it is good enough to represent the point being made. If we assign a probability of failure to each relation or connection, the probability of failure for the entire system increases as the number of parts or nodes increase (because the number of relations increase).

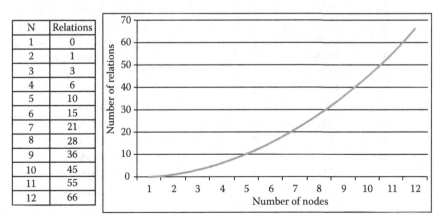

N	Relations
1	0
2	1
3	3
4	6
5	10
6	15
7	21
8	28
9	36
10	45
11	55
12	66

FIGURE 3.2
Example graph for the number of relations based on the number of nodes.

Consider a simple example. Suppose that there are four people working on a project for one month. Assume that as long as these people are working on the project, it will be successful according to its objectives (i.e., the project will be completed on time, on budget, and with all the required scope). If all of them are not available, work cannot proceed, and the project *fails*. Now, suppose that each month, there is a 5% chance that any person will get moved from the project, quit the company, suffer an injury, or in some other way be unable to work. (Again, this is a very simplistic example to illustrate a point and give the readers a feel for the increased chance for failure for larger projects.) In this simple example, there is a small probability that any of the four people will be removed from the project.

In fact, in this simple example, we could mathematically represent the probability of project failure using a binomial distribution. In a binomial distribution, there is a sequence of trials (represented by each person for each month), where each trial is independent, identical, and has the same probability (in this case, 95% probability of success and 5% probability of failure). Table 3.2 shows all the possible outcomes (using an S to indicate a *success* and an F to indicate a *failure*). There are 16 possible outcomes. Only one of these outcomes is complete success: outcome 1 with SSSS.

TABLE 3.2

Probability of Success for Four People Working for One Month

Outcome	Outcome	# of Successes (95%)	# of Failures (5%)	Probability of Outcome
1	SSSS	4	0	81.45%
2	SSSF	3	1	4.29%
3	SSFS	3	1	4.29%
4	SFSS	3	1	4.29%
5	FSSS	3	1	4.29%
6	SSFF	2	2	0.23%
7	SFFS	2	2	0.23%
8	FFSS	2	2	0.23%
9	FSSF	2	2	0.23%
10	SFSF	2	2	0.23%
11	FSFS	2	2	0.23%
12	SFFF	1	3	0.01%
13	FFSF	1	3	0.01%
14	FSFF	1	3	0.01%
15	FFFS	1	3	0.01%
16	FFFF	0	4	0.00%

This outcome has a 81.45% chance of occurring, which means that this simple project has an 18.55% chance of failing (using our simple definition of a project failure).

Now, suppose that the project runs for five months. The number of opportunities for failure rises from 4 (4 people × 1 month = 4) to 20 (4 people × 5 months = 20), and our probability of complete project success (i.e., no failures) drops way down to 35.8%. In other words, there is a 64.2% chance that at least one of the people will be unavailable for at least one month, and, thus, the project will fail. These are not good odds. As stated earlier in the example, this example is not completely correct. Yet, it does serve well to show the power of complexity and opportunities for failures and disconnects for larger projects (which have exponentially more opportunities than small projects).

Why do we care that larger projects suffer failures at a higher rate than smaller projects? It means that the complexity of larger projects introduces elements and considerations that do not exist for smaller projects. Larger projects become their own class of projects and can be treated separately. Thus, all projects are not the same, and special effort and attention need to be provided for larger projects because of the higher degree of difficulty and complexity that is involved. We cannot apply the same thinking that makes small projects successful to the domain of larger and more complex projects. We are doomed to failure with this type of thinking. They are different classes of projects and should be treated as such. To that end, wherever possible, organizations should try to have smaller, more controllable projects. Unfortunately, this is not always possible or feasible. Hence, if a large project is required, then it needs to be planned and managed in a special way.

SOME PROJECT FAILURES ARE PREVENTABLE

Third, it is unanimously agreed that some or possibly many of the reasons projects fail are due to systemic issues. In other words, all projects do not fail because of unforeseen events or incidences beyond the project manager's control or beyond the control of the organization within which the project is taking place. Project failures are not just bad luck. Some of them can be prevented with better practices, better tools, better coordination, etc.

Just about every research report that provides data on project success and failure rates also provides a list of suggestions or recommendations to improve the situation. As with the success and failure rates, it is difficult to find the exact same list across multiple reports. However, there are several common factors that have been cited, although in different reports, they may be described or listed in a different manner. The following is an example list that offers reasons for project failures:

- *The underestimation of complexity, cost, and/or schedule*
- *Failure to establish appropriate control over requirements and/or scope*
- Lack of communications
- Failure to engage stakeholders
- Failure to address culture change issues
- *Lack of oversight/poor project management*
- Poor-quality workmanship
- *Lack of risk management*
- Failure to understand or address system performance requirements
- *Poorly planned or managed transitions*

For the purposes of this book, many of the listed reasons do not directly apply. However, several of these hit upon the same reasons why the authors believe that the current project planning and management tools are insufficient because these tools cannot incorporate some of these dynamics and their impacts. These reasons have been italicized in the preceding list. More details about this will be discussed in Chapters 4 through 6.

In fact, in a companion report to the *classic mistakes* that he listed, Robert Goatham (2015a,b) proposes that dysfunctional and ineffective decision making are the foundation for many project problems. This dysfunctional and ineffective decision making leads to drivers and contributing factors for failures, such as trigger events and behavioral patterns. Ultimately, these drivers and factors create symptoms of failed (or failing) projects that project managers see and respond to (e.g., schedule slippage, budget overruns).

As discussed in Chapter 2, the DPM model within pmBLOX® is based on system dynamics, and more details of this model will be provided in Chapters 5 and 6. As a field, system dynamics puts forth the notion that systems are governed by their underlying structure, and that this structure creates the behaviors that are seen in the system, which results in individual events (Figure 3.3). The authors subscribe to this viewpoint, which is why system dynamics was used as the underlying simulation methodology in pmBLOX. In Figure 3.2, the structure of the system (represented by organizational structure, IT systems, financial processes, and the like) creates

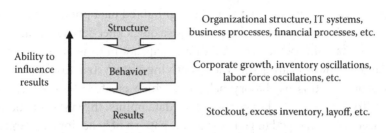

FIGURE 3.3
Structure drives results.

patterns of behavior, such as inventory oscillations or labor force oscillations. The patterns of behavior then create individual events and results
(e.g., inventory stockout, employee layoff). Typically, we tend to react to the
results that we see with a short-term fix to alleviate the *pain* of the event.
The problem with this approach is that the underlying structure is still generating the patterns of behavior that will eventually create the same painful
results or events to which we just reacted. Thus, the true ability to change
and influence the long-term results of a system come from addressing struc-
tural issues. Change the underlying structure, and the results will change.

Figure 3.4 offers a different version of this concept. In Figure 3.3, start
with the single data point on the far right of the graphic. Note that this
is just a snapshot in time, an isolated point. It is human nature to react
quickly to this single data point. However, in this diagram, the pattern of
behavior over time is shown, which in this case is a pattern of oscillation.

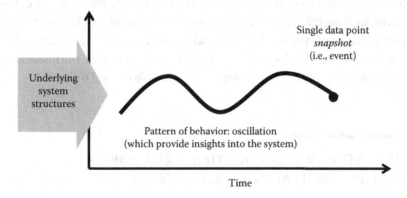

FIGURE 3.4
Structures create patterns of behavior that create single data points.

Values increase for a while and then decrease for a while and then increase again, and so on. By stepping back like this and looking at the pattern of data, it is easy to predict that that the highlighted data point will perhaps change, so there may not be a need to have a quick knee-jerk reaction to the specific data point (which is just a single snapshot in time). On the far left is a large arrow indicating that the underlying system structure is the force that generates this oscillatory behavior, which created the specific data point. To significantly change the future data points, the system structure will need to be changed to generate a new pattern of behavior over time. A good analogy for this is a giant wave pool in a water park. At the back of the pool (behind a large wall) is a structure that quickly pushes down and up in the water. This kicks off a wave that travels through the wave pool. At the *beach* side of the pool, someone standing in the water will have water touching his or her knee at one point and then touching his or her ankle at another point, and the water level oscillates up and down and each wave passes the person standing in the pool. The level of water hitting the person's knee or ankle is the single data point or event. It rises and falls over time due to the oscillatory pattern of behavior of the wave. The structure at the back of the pool generates this oscillation. Stop the structure, and the oscillation stops, which produces a new set of results and data points.

Why do we care that some project failures are systemic in nature? It means that we have an opportunity to change the underlying structure of a project management system to create new patterns of behavior and, ultimately, new results. With the current project planning and management tools, complex projects are treated like simple systems. As pointed out in Chapter 2, this means that the wrong modeling technology is being used, which creates misleading and even incorrect solutions. The evidence of this is in the high degree of project failures that were cited in the "Larger Projects Suffer More Than Smaller Projects" and "Project Failures Are Greater Than Zero" sections in this chapter. To change our project results, the underlying project model needs to change, and this is the role of the DPM.

THE NEED FOR A REVOLUTIONARY PROJECT PLANNING AND MANAGEMENT TOOL

A 2012 survey by the PMI shows that very few companies think that their project management tools are very effective. In fact, nearly half (49%) view them as only moderately effective, and about a quarter (26%) consider them to be completely ineffective. Combined, this means that 75% (three-quarters) of the project managements in the business world do not believe that they are using effective tools. These project managers know that the tools often provide unrealistic results. For example, consider the Microsoft Project issues that were covered in Chapter 1. Many of the readers of this book who use Microsoft Project can probably nod their heads in agreement that those are real issues and that they have to *work around* them all the time. Project managers, including the authors of this book, realize that they have to *game* current tools to get them to produce more realistic and defendable estimates. In other words, the current tools do not produce results and estimates that project managers believe are reasonable, so the project managers make various changes within the tool to force a change in the estimates.

A more recent 2015 report by the PMI states that approximately 29% of project failures came from inadequate cost estimates, 27% of project failures came from inaccurate time estimates, and 23% of project failures came from inadequate resource forecasting. All of these are preventable with better estimates that are provided by a better and more appropriate underlying modeling technology in project planning tools.

So, that begs the question: can project success improve if the tools being used by project managers change? The authors believe that project success can improve with a better modeling technology that is used as the *engine under the hood* for project planning tools (i.e., moving from the CPM to the DPM). That is the crux of the hypothesis for the DARPA research and development effort.

A more realistic representation of the project will impact project success in two major ways. First, the more realistic cost and schedule estimates provided by a DPM-based tool will move the comparison yardstick for a project, which may be enough to make the project successful. For example, suppose that a current CPM-based tool like Microsoft Project indicates that a project can be completed in 10 months for a cost of $1 million. The success of that project will be measured against these two metrics, regardless of how reasonable and realistic these estimates may be. When the project comes in at 12 months and $1.3 million, it will be considered a failure because it took longer and cost more than the original estimates. Using a DPM-based tool like pmBLOX, a new set of cost and schedule estimates would be provided. In this example, suppose that those new estimates are 12 months and $1.4 million. Now, when the project comes in at 12 months and $1.3 million (the exact same final results), the project will be considered a success because it met the original estimates.

Using the example above, it is easy to see that project failures categorized as *schedule slippage* might actually just be a case of having a poor baseline estimate. The original schedule was unachievable, so no wonder the schedule slipped. It had to. And, that probably could have been predicted (and avoided). Project failures categorized as *low quality* might instead be a case of trying to reduce the project scope (i.e., *cut corners*) to meet artificial and unachievable schedule deadlines. Had more realistic schedules been established in the baseline plan, it would have been able to meet all the scope requirements. Project failures categorized as *employee turnover* may be a case of employees getting burned out or fatigued from being pushed so hard (e.g., working lots of overtime) to meet unachievable schedules. And the list goes on. Part of the success of the new Lean- or Agile-based approaches to managing projects is that they use work backlogs (e.g., product backlogs, story backlogs), which are key elements in the DPM. In some cases, the backlogs used in Agile are actual work-hour backlogs (e.g., current sprint encompasses 120 h of work), in which case this becomes exactly like the DPM.

One criticism of the DPM is that it provides estimates that have higher costs and longer schedules. This is a true statement. There are some cases in which the DPM provides a shorter or lower cost estimate than the CPM. But, in most cases, the DPM estimates are higher than the CPM estimates. The criticism is that the DPM costs more and takes longer. This is a ridiculous assertion and makes no sense because the DPM approach is simply providing a more accurate and achievable set of estimates by using a more realistic simulation of the allocation of resources and their accomplishment of work. In our attempt to get things done faster and cheaper, we often sign up to projects with shorter timelines and lower total costs. Just because we want it to take less time and cost less money does not mean that it will. Readers can judge this for themselves based on the discussion in Chapters 5 through 8 that describe the DPM approach and the underlying simulation model in pmBLOX.

A second way that a more realistic representation of the project will impact project success is that a more realistic underlying modeling technology like the DPM can incorporate management decision making that occurs along the progression of a project. What actions will the project manager take if the project is running late or if it is over budget? If the resources are not as productive as originally thought, what is the impact, and what can the project manager do to get the project back on track? The current CPM-based tools provide not only poor estimates for cost and schedules but also one-time static plans that do not teach or guide the project manager on the efficacy of various management actions. For example, if the project is running behind schedule, is it better to assign a little bit of overtime to slowly get the project back on course, or is it better to ramp up the overtime quickly to rapidly get the project back on course? The current tools cannot answer this type of question, but understanding this type of dynamics is paramount to improving one's project management abilities.

Thus, a better tool can educate a project manager on various project dynamics and increase his or her capabilities. With the current tools, a project manager cannot determine if one course of action is better than another. The tools will let the project manager input anything that he or she wants to, regardless of how realistic those inputs are or the negative consequences those inputs may have when implemented in the real world. The current tools do not provide logic checks.

REFERENCES

Devore, J. L. 1991. *Probability and Statistics for Engineering and the Sciences* (3rd edition). Belmont, CA: Brooks/Cole Publishing Company. (ISBN: 0-534-14352-0)

Dorsey, P. 2005. Top 10 reasons why systems projects fail. Dulcian, Inc., April 26. Available at http://www.dulcian.com (accessed February 6, 2015).

Edwards, J., J. Butler, B. Hill, and S. Russell. 1997. *People Rules for Rocket Scientists*. Queensland, Australia: Samford Research Assoc. (ISBN-10: 0646338005)

Goatham, R. 2015a. Classic mistakes (part of the Why Projects Fail blog offered by the International Project Leadership Academy), Calleam Consulting Ltd. Available at http://calleam.com/WTPF/?page_id=799.

Goatham, R. 2015b. Why projects fail (part of the Why Projects Fail blog offered by the International Project Leadership Academy). Calleam Consulting Ltd. Available at http://calleam.com/WTPF/?page_id=2213.

Government Accounting Office. 2015. *Defense Major Automated Information Systems: Cost and Schedule Commitments Need to Be Established Earlier.* Report number GAO-15-282, February 26.

Metcalfe's Law, Wikipedia. Available at https://en.wikipedia.org/wiki/Metcalfe's_law.

Project Management Institute. 2012. *Pulse of the Profession: Driving Success in Challenging Times.* Available at http://www.pmi.org.

Project Management Institute. 2014. *Pulse of the Profession: The High Cost of Low Performance.* Available at http://www.pmi.org.

Project Management Institute. 2015. *Pulse of the Profession: Capturing the Value of Project Management*. Available at http://www.pmi.org.

Senge, P. M. 1990. *The Fifth Discipline: The Art & Practice of the Learning Organization*, New York: Doubleday/Currency.

The Standish Group. 2012. *2012 CHAOS Report*. Available at http://www.standishgroup .com.

4

Critical Path Method and Earned Value Management

Disclaimer: This book and this chapter are not intended to fully teach readers how to use the critical path method (CPM). This book assumes that the readers have some knowledge of the CPM, and (hopefully) they have used the CPM on previous projects. Some basic CPM material is presented to give a landscape against which the DPM will be compared and contrasted. If readers desire to understand more about the CPM, there are many useful resources that are listed in this chapter.

INTRODUCTION

When it was introduced, the CPM was a great improvement in the field of project planning and management. James E. Kelley, Jr. and Morgan R. Walker officially introduced the CPM to the world in an article titled "Critical-path planning and scheduling," published in the March 1959 *Proceedings of the Eastern Joint Computer Conference* (Kelley and Walker, 1959). This article detailed how the CPM was used by DuPont and Remington Rand on the development project for the UNIVersal Automatic Computer I (UNIVAC I) computer beginning in 1957. Prior to this publication, several other types of techniques, tools, and algorithms for project planning and project management had already been introduced (e.g., Gantt chart, flow line scheduling, milestone charts), including elements that became part of the formal CPM approach (e.g., activity on arrow). However, the publication of this article formed the foundation of what we now know as *modern* project management.

CPM REFRESHER

As mentioned at the beginning of this chapter, this book does not intend to provide full training for the CPM or its evolution. This section will provide enough information about the CPM as it is currently understood and implemented (because some elements and techniques of the CPM in the original 1959 article are no longer employed) so that the readers have a background for comparisons to the DPM.

The main objective of the CPM, as its name implies, is to find the *critical path* of tasks or activities through a project, where the critical path is defined as the pathway of interconnected tasks for which there is no (or very little compared to other task pathways) extra time available to perform the tasks. Or, alternatively, the critical path is the pathway of interconnected tasks with the longest duration. In some cases, there may be several critical paths through a project that have no extra time available. In situations like this, the pathway with the longest duration is often considered the critical path. Or, some project managers even choose to have multiple critical paths because they want to highlight all the tasks that must be done to finish the project by its intended end date.

In any case, the main point is that the overall completion of the project is dependent on this critical path (longest duration path). If the tasks on the critical path are delayed, the overall project will also be delayed. Conversely, if the duration of a project needs to be shortened, the first place to start is by reducing the durations of the tasks on the critical path.

To understand enough about the CPM for the readers to compare it to the DPM, a simple example will be used. Figure 4.1 shows a basic network diagram that is used as the starting point for applying the CPM. This is sometimes referred to as the *activity on node* approach because the activity (or task) is represented by a node in the diagram. The arrows are

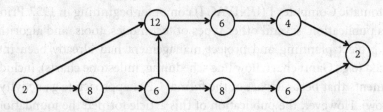

FIGURE 4.1
Network diagram for simple CPM example.

used to show dependencies between tasks. (By comparison, the *activity on arrow* approach uses the arrows to represent the activities themselves, with durations that are specified on the arrows and start or end events that are specified at the nodes.)

It should be noted that in the original CPM approach proposed by Kelley and Morgan, the assumed dependency between tasks was a finish-to-start (FS) dependency. The predecessor task must be complete before the successor task can start. Currently, this has changed so that there are four major types of dependencies between a predecessor task (represented by the first letter) and a successor task (represented by the second letter):

1. *Finish-to-start (FS) (most frequently used)*: The predecessor task must finish before the successor task can start.
2. *Start-to-start (SS)*: Both the predecessor task and the successor task must start at the same time.
3. *Finish-to-finish (FF)*: Both the predecessor task and the successor task must finish at the same time.
4. *Start-to-finish (SF) (very rarely used)*: The predecessor task must start before the successor task can finish.

In addition, there are now *leads* and *lags*, which allow task dependencies to shift a bit. For example, a (FS + 2) dependency indicates that the successor task will start two days *after* (lag) the finish of the predecessor task. A (FS – 2) dependency indicates that the successor task will start two days *before* (lead) the finish of the predecessor task. Readers can find more information about the multitude of variations of task dependencies in other resources. However, this basic information is presented here because it will be referred to later in the book in the discussion of the DPM.

The basic CPM approach has several major steps. There can easily be variations on these steps, but this list covers the basic approach. Figure 4.1 shows the results from the first four activities that are listed as follows:

1. Specify the individual activities.
2. Determine the sequence of those activities.
3. Draw a network diagram.
4. Estimate the completion time for each activity.
5. Identify the critical path (longest path through the network).
6. Update the CPM diagram as the project progresses.

Step 1: Specify the Individual Activities

The first step is to list all activities to be performed on a project. This list can come from the work breakdown structure or a similar document. This listing is then used as the basis for adding sequence and duration information in later steps. In the example in Figure 4.1, there are nine activities to be performed.

Step 2: Determine the Sequence of the Activities

Most tasks on a project are dependent on the completion of other tasks. For each task, make a list of predecessor tasks (i.e., other tasks that must occur prior to this task) and successor tasks (i.e., other tasks that occur after the completion of this task). This information will be used in the next step.

Step 3: Draw a Network Diagram

After defining the dependencies for each task, a network diagram can be drawn. The network diagram is a composite of all of the tasks and their dependencies in a single picture. Figure 4.1 shows the resulting network diagram (also sometimes called a CPM diagram) for our example project. Arrows indicate dependencies with predecessor tasks at the base of the arrow and successor tasks at the head of the arrow.

Step 4: Estimate the Completion Time for Each Activity

The CPM approach does not incorporate uncertainty, so only one number is used to represent the expected duration (or completion time) for each task. In the activity on node approach, the duration for each task is written in the nodes. The duration for each task can be estimated using many different methods: past experience from similar tasks/projects, estimates from knowledgeable people or experts, or best guess, just to name a few. Figure 4.1 shows the network diagram for our example project with durations that are specified for task nodes.

Step 5: Identify the Critical Path

As stated in the "CPM Refresher" section in this chapter, the critical path is the path of tasks through the network that has the longest total duration or, alternatively, no additional time (which is called *slack* or *float*). The significance of the critical path is that if the tasks on the critical path are delayed, the entire project will also be delayed. The critical path is determined through a series of calculations. First, some terms need to be introduced:

- Earliest start time *(ES)*—the earliest time that a task can start. Keep in mind that all predecessor tasks must be completed first.
- Earliest finish time *(EF)*—the earliest time that a task can finish, which is equal to the ES for the task plus the duration for the task.
- Latest finish time *(LF)*—the latest time that a task can finish without delaying the project.
- Latest start time *(LS)*—the latest time that a task can start, which is equal to the LF for the task minus the duration of the task.

Given these definitions, slack time or float can now be defined as the difference between the ES and LS (i.e., LS − ES) or the difference between the EF and LF (i.e., LF − EF). Slack (or float) represents the amount of time that a task can be delayed past the ES without delaying the overall project. The critical path can now be defined as the path of interconnected tasks through a network diagram for which (ES = LS) and (EF = LF) for all the tasks in the path. In other words, the critical path is the set of interconnected tasks for which there is *zero slack* or *zero float*. In this case, a delay in any task in the critical path will delay the overall project. In Figure 4.2, ES, EF, LS, and LF are shown in quadrants for each task, with the key being in the upper left of the figure.

To calculate the ES values for each task, begin with the first task of the project. In Figures 4.1 and 4.2, this is the node that is farthest to the left (since work flows left to right in the diagram). The earliest time that the first task can start is the beginning of day 1 (ES = 1). Since it has a duration of 2 days, the earliest time that the first task can finish is the end of day 2 (EF = 2). Now, follow the

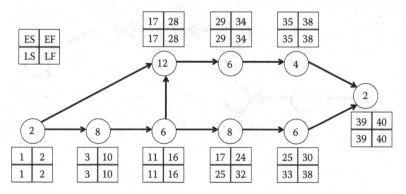

FIGURE 4.2
CPM example with ES, EF, LS, and LF values.

arrows from the first task. The earliest time that the second task (which has a duration of 8 days) can start is the beginning of day 3 (ES = 3), and the earliest time that it can finish is the end of day 10 (EF = 10). Continuing along the line of arrows at the bottom of the diagram, the third task (which has a duration of 6 days) can start as early as the beginning of day 11 (ES = 11) and can finish as early as the end of day 16 (EF = 16). Notice that from this third task, there are two arrows: one going up to a task with a duration of 12 days and one going to the right to a task with a duration of 8 days. Notice also that the task with the duration of 12 days follows the first task (duration of 2 days). The earliest time that the 12-day task can start is *not* immediately after the first task finishes but instead is after the third task finishes because of the dependency on the third task, too. Thus, the 12-day task and 8-day tasks both have an early start time of the beginning of day 17 (ES = 17). This process of calculating the ES and EF for each task is continued throughout the rest of the project, as shown in Figure 4.2. The earliest time that the entire project can finish is the end of day 40 (EF = 40), as seen on the far right of the network diagram.

At this point, the ES and EF values for each task have been calculated. This is often called the *forward pass* calculation through the network diagram. To calculate the LS and LF values, we do a *backward pass* calculation starting from the final task and working backward (right to left in Figure 4.2). For the final task, the latest finish time is the same as the earliest finish time (i.e., LF = EF), unless another due date is known. In this case, it is day 40. After working backward from the end of the project to the beginning of the project, we can now see the critical path, as highlighted in Figure 4.3. On the critical path, each task has ES = LS (and EF = LF).

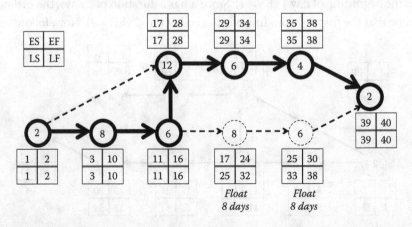

FIGURE 4.3
CPM example with critical path highlighted.

In this simple example, there are only two tasks that do not fall on the critical path. Obviously, for larger and more complex projects, there will be many more tasks that do not fall on the critical path.

Step 6: Update the CPM Diagram as the Project Progresses

As the days go by, and the project progresses, the actual task completion times will be known for many of the tasks. Consequently, the network diagram can be updated with these days/times. If any of these actual start or finish times changed from the planned start or finish times, a new critical path may emerge. If this happens, adjustments may be necessary to the project to get it back on schedule. These adjustments would start with focusing on the tasks on the critical path to see where these tasks could be shortened or even removed (which may result in a new network diagram with a different structure from the original network diagram).

The six steps represent the major activities that are conducted in a CPM analysis for a project. As can be seen, this process can be conducted manually, if needed, with pencil and paper. However, there are plenty of currently available software programs that do all this work automatically. One software tool that will be mentioned quite often in this book is Microsoft Project, but there are many more. Due to the ubiquity of Microsoft Office products for many organizations, Microsoft Project is one of the most common off-the-shelf project planning tools, and it provides a good point of comparison as the DPM is discussed.

SOME COMMENTS ON PROGRAM EVALUATION AND REVIEW TECHNIQUE

It should be noted that the program evaluation and review technique (PERT), developed around the same time as the CPM by Booz Allen Hamilton, the Lockheed Missile System Division, and the US Navy for the Polaris submarine missile program, is another popular project planning and management approach that is often used in conjunction with the CPM. It is not uncommon to see the term PERT/CPM being used to refer to the combined approach. Similar to the CPM, the PERT also incorporates the concept of a critical path, and many of the calculations are the exact same.

The major difference with the PERT is that task durations are assigned three values: (1) most likely time (M), (2) optimistic time (O), and (3) pessimistic time (P). Or, sometimes, these are referred to as *most likely*, *best-case*, and *worst-case* times. These different times or durations are used to account for uncertainty: we do not know with exact precision how long a task will take (since we have not done it yet). The PERT then calculates the *expected time* (duration) for a task to be the following:

$$\text{Expected time} = (O + 4M + P)/6.$$

For example, suppose that the most likely duration for a task is 8 days (M = 8), the optimistic duration is 6 days (O = 6), and the pessimistic duration is 16 days (P = 16). Then, the expected duration would be the following:

$$
\begin{aligned}
\text{Expected time} &= (O + 4M + P)/6 \\
&= (6 + 4 \times 8 + 16)/6 \\
&= 54/6 \\
&= 9 \text{ days.}
\end{aligned}
$$

The readers will notice that this formula essentially gives the most weight to the *most likely* duration for the task, but it includes a little weighting for the best possible duration and the worst possible duration. It is sort of like hedging a bet. Because of uncertainty, we think that a task will have a particular duration (most likely), but, just in case it does not happen that way, let us modify our expectation for planning purposes. Depending on the planner's confidence in the three different values, the weighting may change. For example, if a project planner wanted to allow the pessimistic (or worst-case) value to have a stronger impact, then the following formula may be used:

$$\text{Expected time} = (O + 3M + 2P)/6.$$

In our example above, this would provide a new expected duration that is longer than the original:

$$\text{Expected time} = (O + 3M + 2P)/6$$

$$= (6 + 3 \times 8 + 2 \times 16)/6$$

$$= 62/6$$

$$= 10.33 \text{ days.}$$

This expected time, or expected duration, is then used within a CPM-type approach. Of course, there could be many different variations, but, in the end, the PERT simply tries to provide a more realistic value for the duration of a task. For example, the expected durations for each task would be included in the nodes in Figures 4.1 through 4.3. *The key point is that the PERT/CPM is a duration-based approach that uses task durations as the foundation for planning.* This key fact will be highlighted throughout the remainder of this book.

BENEFITS AND DISADVANTAGES OF PERT/CPM

The PERT/CPM was a great innovation when it was introduced. It provided many benefits, such as

- Visualizing the interdependency of tasks (through the network diagram)
- Highlighting task priorities (through the use of the critical path)
- Showing where parallel activities are possible (i.e., not on the critical path)
- Calculating the shortest duration that is expected for a project

At the time, these were great steps forward in management capabilities. The benefits far outweighed the weaknesses. However, currently, our level of sophistication is such that the scale has tipped, and the disadvantages and weaknesses of the PERT/CPM are significant enough to outweigh the benefits. Fundamentally, the PERT/CPM approach suffers from three major flaws:

1. Task duration is an input.
2. Resource productivity impacts are not considered.
3. Management corrective actions are not captured.

Task Duration Is an Input

As seen in the "Some Comments on Program Evaluation and Review Technique" section in this chapter, in the PERT/CPM, the duration of a task is used as the primary input. However, many factors (e.g., availability and productivity of resources, dependencies among tasks, hours worked by employees) affect the duration of a task. Thus, in the real world, task duration is actually an *output*. We do not know the actual duration until the work is complete.

For instance, based on the fact that durations are used as the foundation for planning in the PERT/CPM, a full plan can be developed with questionable and unrealistic task durations. This is a huge risk for projects: to start with an unrealistic baseline plan. For large projects, the details for how durations were estimated can be lost or difficult to recover, so many of the task durations could be suspicious to begin with. Even worse, in some cases, durations are created to meet other external requirements, and the resulting durations may or may not be possible or practical. The point here is that, as much as planners and managers may try to be objective in their estimates, many estimates for task durations are subjective to fit the situation. For example, on a project that one of the authors was planning at a major defense company, the author was told by his superior to create a plan that started on day X and ended on day Y. There was no concern for realistic estimates. Durations were created to make sure that the start date and end date matched the superior's demands. All the while, the author knew that this was a completely unrealistic plan that had many faulty (yet convenient and plausible) assumptions. In effect, it was doomed from the beginning. This may sound terrible, but it is a more common occurrence than readers may realize. Or, if the reader has been in the project management field for quite some time, he or she probably has similar stories to tell in which the realism of the duration estimates was set aside for some other higher priority.

Instead, the DPM put forward the notion that the application and use of resources should serve as the fundamental inputs for project planning. Are resources even available? If so, how many are available? Are there enough? If there are not enough, how does this constrain the completion of tasks? Are key resources shared across multiple tasks that must be completed simultaneously? From just this short list of questions, it is easy to see how the availability and sharing of resources (including people, materials, and equipment) can significantly alter the expected durations for tasks and, ultimately, the duration for the entire project.

Resource Productivity Impacts Are Not Considered

If resources are used as the inputs for tasks, one of the first questions that must be asked is, "How much work can these resources do in a given amount of time?" This relates to resource *productivity*. As used here, the term productivity covers all aspects of getting work done in a specific period of time. First, productivity can apply to the speed at which work is done. For example, one person may be able to lay 1000 ft.² of carpet in an hour, and another person may be able to lay 5000 ft.² of carpet in an hour. Or, one machine may be able to produce 60 parts in an hour, and another machine may be able to produce the same part at a rate of 120 parts per hour. Second, productivity can apply to the total work done, or *work throughput*, which may include rework. For instance, two people can work at the same rate (e.g., 10 documents per hour), but one person may make more mistakes than the other person, and, therefore, this first person must spend more time fixing the mistakes (i.e., rework). In an hour, the first person may only get six documents completely finished, so this person's resulting productivity is six documents per hour. The second person, making fewer mistakes and requiring less rework, may have a resulting productivity of nine documents per hour.

Most current PERT/CPM project planning tools available exacerbate the issues that are related to a nonresource focus. In many PERT/CPM tools, resources can be added to or removed from a task with no impact on the productivity of labor that is applied to the task. The current tools assume that all resources are equal. Yet, we know that they are not. New employees or junior-level employees do not get as much work done in the same period of time as experienced, senior-level employees. Also, in current PERT/CPM tools, people can be scheduled for overtime with no impact on their productivity. However, anyone who has worked a significant amount of overtime can validate that productivity decreases due to fatigue or burnout. Working a little overtime for a couple of days usually has a negligible impact, but long periods of working overtime can have significant impacts on labor productivity. Lastly, it is a commonly accepted fact (especially on software development projects) that throwing more people at a task often makes the task fall further behind schedule due to lower labor productivity, as experienced people train the new people, and the new people make mistakes that must be corrected. However, in many PERT/CPM tools, resources are handled rather simply. For example, the duration for a project can be cut in half by doubling the resources.

Taken to the extreme, this means that the duration for a project can be cut to 1% of the original duration if 100 times (100×) the resources are used. Many people refer to this fallacy with the adage, "Nine women cannot have a baby in one month." In some cases, just based on the work to be done, adding people does not considerably shorten the duration of the job. If there are physical space requirements (e.g., working in a confined space), it may limit the amount of resources that can be applied (e.g., only 2 plumbers can fit in the space under a sink, not 10 plumbers).

It should be noted that some current PERT/CPM project planning tools attempt to account for the impact of resources. For instance, in addition to allowing duration inputs for tasks, Microsoft Project has an option for *effort-driven* tasks, which treats the task work as a backlog of work to be done. More will be said about this in the description of the DPM in Chapters 5 through 8.

Management Corrective Actions Are Not Captured

The actual management decisions and actions that project managers take during a project are not included in the PERT/CPM. However, these corrective actions can significantly influence progress, which means that they can significantly impact any project planning. Current PERT/CPM planning tools only match resources against task assignments. As a result, these tools allow for static planning but not dynamic reaction and replanning. In current project planning and management tools, if it looks like a task will run late (e.g., based on the earned-value schedule performance index [SPI]), the project manager must manually develop several different plans through trial and error to see if they will work. The current tools do not help the project manager actually manage the project or show the consequences of management decisions. The tools only allow the project manager to develop multiple, static plans with no insight. Since almost every project requires some sort of corrective action, it is imperative that the planning and management approach employed by the project manager and team somehow incorporates these corrective actions. Specifically, when should these corrective actions occur, which corrective actions will occur, and how aggressively should these corrective actions be applied?

These inherent flaws indicate that the *modern* PERT/CPM approach itself and the software tools based on the PERT/CPM are too simplistic and do not reflect reality. As a result, these tools cause project managers and teams to make decisions that are detrimental to project success. In fact, it is not uncommon to doom a project to failure (or at least a very long and difficult road) with the *very first baseline project plan*. In other words, right out of the gate, the project is already off course. This is not a criticism of project managers; it is rather a criticism of the simplistic approaches that are found in current PERT/CPM-based planning and management tools that give us insufficient and sometimes even incorrect answers. Consequently, we often rely heavily on individual project managers to single-handedly make projects successful. We applaud heroic efforts in which project managers work around the *system* to make everything work out right. Why not have a system that actually helps the project team succeed?

Essentially, the current planning tools are not capable of handling the complexity of the issues that are experienced on most projects today because they are rooted in a simplistic approach that was developed over 60 years ago. When it was developed, the PERT/CPM approach was innovative and useful. Unfortunately, its effectiveness and appropriateness have significantly eroded over time. If we want a better tool for managing projects, we need a better approach than the PERT/CPM.

SOME COMMENTS ON CRITICAL CHAIN

The critical chain approach, developed by Eliyahu M. Goldratt and published in his book *Critical Chain* (Goldratt, 1997), is the most recent improvement to the CPM and attempts to solve some of CPM's shortcomings. Similar to the disclaimer above for the short coverage of the CPM, this part of the chapter will not attempt to teach critical chain in its entirety. Only key points will be highlighted.

The first major difference with critical chain relates to estimates for task durations. In the critical chain approach, it is assumed that *safety* time is built into every duration estimate because of the uncertainty of how long the task will actually take and because there is a desire to make sure that the task is completed within the declared duration. Like the changes made with the PERT, this assumption tries to arrive at better duration estimates. (Thus, notice that this is still a duration-based approach.) Typically, this safety time is on the order of 100% of the actual time. (Or, another way of saying this is that the true duration is typically 50% of the stated duration.) For instance, if someone states that his or her task will take eight days, it typically will only take four days, with the other four days being safety time to reduce the risk of being late. The critical chain approach essentially uses Parkinson's law that every activity will expand to fill the entire time that is allotted for it (Parkinson, 1955). If a project manager tells someone that he or she has eight days to finish the task, that person will take eight days (even if he or she could do it in only four days). In this example, if the safety time is stripped away, and the person is told that he or she only has four days to complete the task, that person will (most likely) be able to do it in four days. And, now the project manager has gained four extra days.

This extra time will be used as *buffers* at different places in the project plan. A key point here is that critical chain uses these buffers to manage and control the project instead of task progress reports. Since the exact duration for any task is unknown, then it is useless to manage tasks to an *exact end time*. Instead, the remaining time in the buffers is used to measure the status and health of the project.

For example, one issue with the PERT/CPM that causes problems is the concept of a late start. On any noncritical path, there is slack time or float time (float = LS – ES). If a task waits until the late start time to actually start, there is no more float time, and that task is *now on the critical path* because it has no extra time. By using up float time, project managers can *inadvertently create* additional critical paths. Critical chain addresses this by putting *feeding buffers* at the end of each string of tasks that feed into the critical path. For the critical path, the additional time is placed at the end of the project and called the *project buffer*. Figure 4.4 provides a critical chain view of the same CPM example that was used in Figure 4.3. Notice that the overall duration of the critical path is now 20 days (50% of the original 40 days), and the remaining 20 days is captured in a project buffer at the end of the project. Similarly, on noncritical path

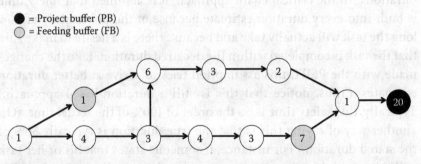

● = Project buffer (PB)
○ = Feeding buffer (FB)

FIGURE 4.4
CPM example with critical chain elements added.

segments, the additional time is captured as feeding buffers prior to the segment's connection to the critical path.

The reader will notice that the use of buffers applies to the first flaw of the PERT/CPM that was stated in the "Benefits and Disadvantages of PERT/CPM" section of this chapter: task durations are uncertain (because the durations are outputs in the real world, not inputs). Critical chain chooses to address this uncertainty by forcing shorter durations on tasks (i.e., 50% of the stated duration) and using buffers to capture extra time. The DPM chooses to address this uncertainty by completely eliminating the input of durations at all and instead simulating the use of resources to determine appropriate durations.

The second major difference with critical chain is a focus on resources. In fact, this is where critical chain gets its name. The critical chain is the longest pathway of tasks through the project based on both task dependencies and resource dependencies (i.e., tasks that share the same resource, even if those tasks are not in sequence with each other). If resources are unlimited, then the critical chain is equivalent to the critical path. However, in most realistic cases, the resources are not unlimited, and, therefore, the limited resources cause the project to be constrained. This causes the pathway with the most constraints (and, thus, the longest time) to possibly be different from the critical path that is derived through the traditional PERT/CPM approach.

The objective of critical chain is to shift tasks so that key resources are not needed simultaneously on multiple tasks. With limited resources, this almost always results in one of the tasks being late because the key resource is working on another task. However, if tasks and feeding buffers are moved around, it is usually possible to resolve these resource conflicts. Within critical chain, this is also referred to as resource leveling: create a work plan for constrained resources that shifts work so that the resource only works the typical workday (e.g., 8 h/day).

To see how this works in practice, look at Figure 4.5. In this example, we assume that the same resource is needed in several tasks, and, to make it even simpler, let us assume that this resource is a single person (denoted by "X"). Figure 4.5 presents the four tasks that use resource X. Figure 4.6 shows how feeding buffers are moved, and the resulting critical chain highlighted with thick, dotted arrows (which is different from the critical path that is highlighted in Figure 4.3).

The reader will notice that the focus on resources in critical chain applies to the first two major flaws of the PERT/CPM that are stated in

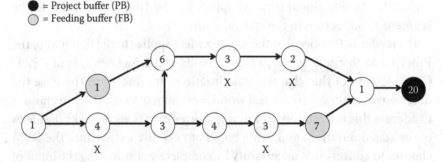

FIGURE 4.5
Tasks using resource X.

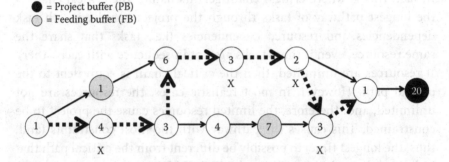

FIGURE 4.6
Critical chain through project.

the "Benefits and Disadvantages of PERT/CPM" section of this chapter. The utilization of resources has a direct impact on task durations. Critical chain chooses to address this through manual methods of shifting tasks on the project network diagram and managing and shifting resources around. The DPM selects to address this by simulating the actual utilization of resources.

Critical chain definitely makes some needed improvements to the PERT/CPM by showing the importance of resource constraints and their impact on the critical path for a project. However, critical chain is still a duration-based approach that uses duration as an input, albeit with some changes to the durations to decrease the risk of the project running late. As the reader will see in later chapters, the DPM takes this resource-based focus further through operational simulation of resource utilization.

UNCERTAINTY AND MONTE CARLO ANALYSIS

Durations (when used as inputs) are uncertain. They are estimates. But, what if the estimates are not exactly correct? One way to deal with this is the PERT method of estimating a duration based on best-case, most likely, and worst-case durations. Another more sophisticated method is Monte Carlo analysis. This analysis (also known as Monte Carlo simulation) is used to understand the *realm of possible outcomes* when the input data are uncertain for a project plan. It is a process by which a simulation is run hundreds or even thousands of times, with slight variations of the inputs for each simulation run. In the end, statistics are provided that show the average and minimum (min) or maximum (max) range for various outputs, along with other statistical information (e.g., standard deviation). Let us consider a very simple example to understand the process behind Monte Carlo analysis.

In a duration-based estimating approach (e.g., PERT/CPM), the inputs are the durations of tasks. Suppose that there is a project that is composed of two tasks, in which Task 1 has an estimated duration of 10 days, and Task 2 has an estimated duration of 5 days. Task 1 must be complete before Task 2 can start (i.e., finish-to-start dependency). In this simple example (Figure 4.7, for now disregard the DPM information), it is easy to determine that the total estimated duration is 15 days (10 days + 5 days = 15 days). However, suppose that the project planner is uncertain of the true

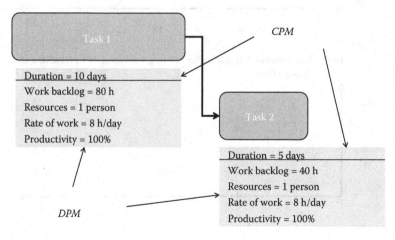

FIGURE 4.7
Simple Monte Carlo example.

durations of Tasks 1 and 2. The duration of Task 1 could actually be anywhere from 8 to 12 days, with an equal probability of being any duration between 8 and 12 days (Figure 4.8). The planner just picked the duration of 10 days for Task 1 because it was in the middle. The duration of Task 2 could either be 4 or 5 days, with a 75% probability of being 4 days and a 25% probability of being 5 days (Figure 4.8). The planner just picked the duration of 5 days because it was the *safest* choice.

A Monte Carlo analysis of this project would run this project hundreds or thousands of times, changing the durations for Tasks 1 and 2 based on the probabilities that were given. At the end, the analysis would provide statistics for all the new total durations for the project. This is called a distribution. Just by looking at the ranges of durations for the two tasks, we can quickly figure out Table 4.1.

What we do not know are the probabilities of achieving each of these durations, along with the probabilities of achieving any duration in between the min and max durations. This is the information that is provided by the Monte Carlo analysis. Table 4.2 provides the results from

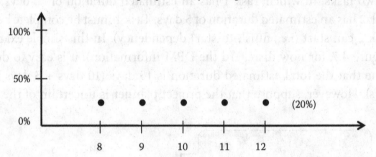

Task 1: Duration has equal probability of being between 8 and 12 days.

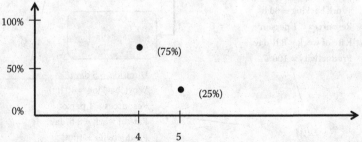

Task 2: Duration has 75% probability of being 4 days and 25% probability of being 5 days.

FIGURE 4.8
Probabilities of various durations for each task.

TABLE 4.1

Basic Duration Estimates with CPM

	Min Duration	**Expected Duration**	**Max Duration**
Task 1	8 days	10 days	12 days
Task 2	4 days	5 days	5 days
Total project	12 days	15 days	17 days

TABLE 4.2

Results of Monte Carlo Analysis
with Durations

Total Duration	**Probability**
12 days	17.5%
13 days	18.0%
14 days	19.5%
15 days	16.0%
16 days	4.5%
17 days	24.5%
	100%

200 simulation runs using Microsoft Excel. Notice that the probability of achieving 15 days (the expected duration) is only 16%. In fact, in this example, there is a 29% chance that the project will run longer than 15 days (4.5% + 24.5% = 29%). Furthermore, there is a 55% chance that the project will run shorter than 15 days (17.5% + 18% + 19.5% = 55%).

In a resource-based estimating approach (e.g., DPM), the inputs are based on resource information (Figure 4.7, now look at the DPM information). Staying with the simple example from above, suppose that the estimated duration of 10 days for Task 1 was based on one person working at an assumed level of productivity of 100% for 8 h each day, and the amount of work to do for Task 1 was 80 h. The equation for duration would be the following:

$$\text{Duration} = (\text{amount of work to do})/(\text{work completed per day})$$

$$= (80\,\text{h})/([1\,\text{person}] \times [100\%\,\text{productivity}] \times [8\,\text{h/day}])$$

$$= (80\,\text{h})/(8\,\text{h/day})$$

$$= 10\,\text{days}.$$

Suppose that the estimated duration of 5 days for Task 2 was also based on one person working at an assumed level of productivity of 100% for 8 h each day, and the amount of work to do for Task 2 was 40 h. The equation for duration would be the following:

$$\text{Duration} = (\text{amount of work to do})/(\text{work completed per day})$$

$$= (40\,\text{h})/([1\,\text{person}]\times[100\%\,\text{productivity}]\times[8\,\text{h/day}])$$

$$= (40\,\text{h})/(8\,\text{h/day})$$

$$= 5\,\text{days}.$$

If Monte Carlo analysis is applied to the resource-based approach, the uncertainty of inputs is now at the resource level. For example, suppose that the availability of these resources could be anything from 6 to 9 h/day (i.e., equal probability of each number), and assume that the productivity level of these resources could be anything from 75% to 100% (i.e., equal probability of each level) (Figure 4.9).

As with the duration-based example, we can quickly figure out the min or max durations for each task as follows:

Task 1

$$\text{Min duration} = (\text{amount of work to do})/(\text{work completed per day})$$

$$= (80\,\text{h})/([1\,\text{person}]\times[100\%\,\text{productivity}]\times[9\,\text{h/day}])$$

$$= (80\,\text{h})/(9\,\text{h/day})$$

$$= 8.9\,\text{days}.$$

$$\text{Max duration} = (\text{amount of work to do})/(\text{work completed per day})$$

$$= (80\,\text{h})/([1\,\text{person}]\times[75\%\,\text{productivity}]\times[6\,\text{h/day}])$$

$$= (80\,\text{h})/(4.5\,\text{h/day})$$

$$= 17.8\,\text{days}.$$

Task 2

$$\text{Min duration} = (\text{amount of work to do})/(\text{work completed per day})$$

$$= (40\,\text{h})/([1\,\text{person}]\times[100\%\,\text{productivity}]\times[9\,\text{h/day}])$$

$$= (40\,\text{h})/(9\,\text{h/day})$$

$$= 4.4\,\text{days}.$$

Availability: Resource has equal probability of being available 6–9 h/day.

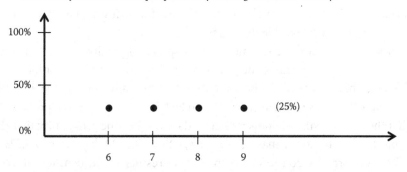

Productivity: Resource has equal probability of being 75%–100% productive.

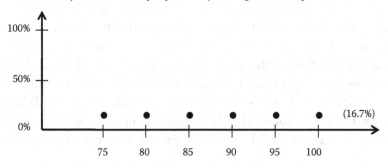

FIGURE 4.9
Probabilities of various resource inputs for each task.

$$\text{Min duration} = (\text{amount of work to do})/(\text{work completed per day})$$

$$= (40\,\text{h})/([1\,\text{person}] \times [75\%\,\text{productivity}] \times [6\,\text{h/day}])$$

$$= (40\,\text{h})/(4.5\,\text{h/day})$$

$$= 8.9\,\text{days}.$$

The min/max/expected durations are given in Table 4.3.

TABLE 4.3

Basic Duration Estimates with DPM

	Min Duration	**Expected Duration**	**Max Duration**
Task 1	8.9 days	10 days	17.8 days
Task 2	4.4 days	5 days	8.9 days
Total project	13.3 days	15 days	26.7 days

Assuming equal probabilities of all hours per day and all productivity levels, the Monte Carlo analysis provides the following probabilistic information regarding possible durations (Table 4.4).

First, notice that there is a much wider spread of possible durations when Monte Carlo is applied at the resource level instead of the duration level. Second, this means that the probability of actually hitting the initially expected 15 days is much lower (9.5%). In fact, in this example, the probability that the project will run longer than 15 days is 86%. The probability that the project will run shorter than 15 days (i.e., either 13 or 14 days) is only 4.5%.

The resource-based Monte Carlo analysis results are quite different from the duration-based Monte Carlo analysis results above, and these differences come mainly from the location of the uncertainty. In the duration-based approach, the uncertainty is suffered at the duration level. In the resource-based approach, the uncertainty is suffered at the resource level. Figure 4.10 summarizes the results of both of the Monte Carlo analyses.

This simple example is used to emphasize the differences in results that are obtained from a duration-based approach (like PERT/CPM) and a resource-based approach (like the DPM). Because of these differences, a project manager would have a different set of priorities to act upon

TABLE 4.4

Results of Monte Carlo Analysis with Resources

Total Duration	Probability
13 days	0.0%
14 days	4.5%
15 days	9.5%
16 days	5.5%
17 days	3.0%
18 days	14.5%
19 days	11.0%
20 days	7.5%
21 days	10.0%
22 days	9.0%
23 days	6.5%
24 days	9.0%
25 days	4.0%
26 days	1.5%
27 days	4.5%
	100%

Probability of being	*CPM*	*DPM*
Shorter than planned	55%	4.5%
Exactly as planned	16%	9.5%
Longer than planned	29%	86%

FIGURE 4.10
Comparison of Monte Carlo simulations for duration-based approach (CPM) and resource-based approach (DPM).

depending on which approach was used. The DPM makes the argument, similar to critical chain, that the utilization of resources and the constraints associated with these resources are key elements to understanding how to manage projects effectively and successfully.

ADDITIONAL ISSUES WITH PERT/CPM

As stated in the "Benefits and Disadvantages of PERT/CPM" section in this chapter, a list of three major flaws was provided for the PERT/CPM:

1. Task duration is an input.
2. Resource productivity impacts are not considered.
3. Management corrective actions are not captured.

While these are the major issues with the PERT/CPM, there are several additional minor issues that also exist.

The first minor issue is based on the simplicity of the approach. With the ubiquity of the PERT/CPM, many software companies have created planning tools that are based on the PERT/CPM. One feature that is often highlighted to help with marketability is the user-friendliness of a planning tool. The makers will say that the tool is so easy to use that even a beginner can use it like a professional. This allows inexperienced project managers to form plans based on their limited knowledge of activities and resources. Because it is fairly easy to create a project in these tools and just define the durations for tasks, anyone and everyone thinks that they can schedule projects because the tools are so easy to use. This adds to the risk of creating an unrealistic (or even impossible) baseline project plan. Many times, a project manager is told by a higher authority that a project must start on an x date and end on a y date. No ifs, ands, or buts. So, the project manager simply creates a plan that does, indeed, start on an x date and end on a y date. The whole time, he or she is well aware that these dates are highly unlikely, if not unachievable. But, it is easier to make everyone happy and give the appearance of potential success. Then, when the project has already progressed a few weeks, and everyone realizes that the project is behind schedule (because of the unrealistic initial plan), the finger-pointing can start, and the lateness can be blamed on many other things so that no one takes the fall. In an effort to correct the situation, another minor issue arises.

The second minor issue is that common *fixes* for projects, such as *fast-tracking* (performing more activities in parallel) and *crashing the project* (shortening the durations of tasks on the critical path by adding resources), cannot be validated in most PERT/CPM tools. These additional fixes often make the project perform even more poorly, that is, they add to the problem of being behind schedule (or being over budget) instead of actually fixing it. While fast-tracking and crashing are common approaches, with PERT/CPM tools, it is impossible to understand the true impact of these corrective actions. PERT/CPM tools make these approaches look convincing and completely doable. Let us take crashing as an example. In a PERT/CPM tool, the duration for a project can be cut in half by doubling the resources that are assigned to it. This is completely unreasonable and very misleading. While it may be true for some types of work, for most it is not. Consequently, along with unrealistic baseline plans, PERT/CPM tools can also provide unrealistic fixes to performance problems, which exacerbate the original problems and take the project farther and farther from any realistic option. This only makes a project manager fast-track and crash the project even more, leading to more problems. It can quickly become a vicious, downward cycle.

The third minor issue relates to resource leveling. With PERT/CPM tools, it is easy to set durations without concern for the use of resources. When resources are allocated to tasks, to maintain the original durations, these resources are often overallocated. This means that the resources are worked more than 8 h/day (or whatever the normal workday is for the project). For example, a resource may show 200% allocation, which means that the resource must work 16 h/day (or twice whatever the normal workday is for the project). (As a side note, overallocation occurs because duration is actually disconnected from resource usage. The allocation of resources to tasks in PERT/CPM tools does not mean that there is any true assignment. Resources can be allocated at any level, and durations can be set to any length without any consistent logic.) To correct resource overallocations in PERT/CPM tools, resources can be *leveled*, which means that the work is spread out to limit the resource so that it works only on the normal workday (e.g., 8 h/day). However, sometimes, the algorithms used by the PERT/CPM tools for resource leveling can provide inconsistent (and sometimes incorrect) answers.

For example, Figure 4.11 shows the results from different versions of the same project plan in Microsoft Project. The plan is for the development of an aircraft sensor for a large defense contractor. The top bar is the original (overallocated) plan, which is known to be overly optimistic and unrealistic. It shows that the project will take a little over 3 years at a total cost of $13.1 million. The second bar shows that when the resources are leveled on a weekly basis, the plan stretches out to 50 years. When the plan is scrutinized, it shows that work is done for the first few years, then the resources sit idle for about 40 years, and then the resources are used again. And, amazingly, the cost is the same: $13.1 million. Clearly, this is too pessimistic and, again, unrealistic. In fact, it is outright incorrect. In the third bar, the resources are then leveled on a monthly basis, and the duration is shown to be about 6.5 years at the same $13.1-million cost. At this point, it is difficult to trust the answers that are provided by the tool because the weekly leveled plan is so wrong. In the end, all three of these plans are quite useless to a project manager. Yet, one of them has to be used. The project manager has a real dilemma on his or her hands.

The fourth issue relates to project performance along cost and schedule dimensions. With the PERT/CPM, there is no information that shows the current status of the project with regards to the planned cost and planned schedule (duration) for the project. The PERT/CPM is primarily used for

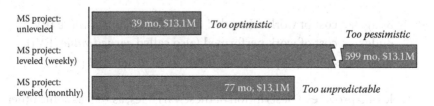

FIGURE 4.11
Resource leveling example.

baseline project planning before the project starts. While the PERT/CPM can be utilized for project monitoring and control, it is extremely difficult. And, similar to the other issues cited in this chapter for the inadequacy of the PERT/CPM to show true performance consequences, any updated plan still suffers from a lack of realism. Just like the baseline plans are risky because we are not sure if the project resources can actually accomplish the work in the time frame that is specified, updated plans using the PERT/CPM are equally risky with their illusions of *improved performance* for the projects.

Currently, *earned value* (EV, also called *earned value management* [EVM]) is the only formal, standardized approach for evaluating the schedule and cost performance for a project. EV definitely has its own shortcomings. However, since it is the only formalized approach in widespread use, it will be the basis for this book. With the current PERT/CPM tools, there are often add-on tools or third-party tools that conduct EV analysis. Thus, project status information may be present within some PERT/CPM tools, but this is not a formal part of the PERT/CPM. EV requires information about work progress on each task (i.e., how much work has been done so far and how much work still remains). The duration-based approach of the PERT/CPM does not adequately capture this information in any standard way.

EV REFRESHER

Similar to the CPM refresher at the beginning of this chapter, this book does not intend to provide full training for EV techniques. This section will provide enough information about EV so that the reader has a background for what EV is, how EV is not included in the PERT/CPM, and how EV is used within a DPM framework.

EV attempts to compare *work performed* versus *work planned*. There are three key independent variables that are used in EV:

1. Budgeted cost of work scheduled (also called *planned value* [PV])
2. Budgeted cost of work performed (also called *earned value* [EV])
3. Actual cost of work performed (also called *actual cost* [AC])

Tables 4.5 provides a description of these variables, as well as some other variables. Table 4.6 presents a description of some key EV metrics that are

TABLE 4.5

Key EV Variables

Variable	Description	Meaning
BCWS (PV)	The budgeted cost of work scheduled (BCWS) is the dollarized value of all the work that is scheduled to be accomplished in a given period of time. The BCWS is the planning function that is required by earned value and establishes the baseline against which performance is measured.	Planning baseline
BCWP (EV)	The budgeted cost of work performed (BCWP) is the dollarized value of all the work that is actually accomplished in a given period of time. The variable is also called earned value and symbolizes the completion of work. The BCWP is not realized until the work is completed.	Work accomplishment, earned value
ACWP (AC)	The actual cost of work performed (ACWP) is the cost that is incurred and recorded for performance measurement purposes within a given period of time. The ACWP is independently reported by the contractor's accounting system.	Expenditures
BaC	The budget at completions (BaCs) are established early in the project for every given level of the work breakdown structure. They capture the budgets for all authorized work, and they are the benchmarks for forecasting overruns and underruns.	Authorized work
EaC	The estimate at completions (EaCs) are an independent forecast of the final costs that are required to complete any given level of the work breakdown structure. These are normally reported by the contractor. The contractor's EAC is also called the latest revised estimate.	Forecast cost

calculated based on the variables in Table 4.5. *Note*: There are several more metrics that are used in the full implementation of EV for a project.

The following tables and charts put forth a simple example that shows EV calculations. In Table 4.7, two projects are compared. Both share the same baseline plan, shown in the first two columns. The projects are both 10 months in duration with a total estimated cost of $1000. Notice, however, that the accumulation rate for costs is not linear (i.e., $100 per month over 10 months). Months 3–7 have amounts that are different from

TABLE 4.6

Key EV Metrics

Metric	Description	Meaning
SV = BCWP – BCWS (SV = EV – PV)	Schedule variance (SV) indicates that some amount of work was not completed as originally planned. A positive SV indicates that the work was completed ahead of the original plan. A negative SV indicates that the work was not completed on time as originally scheduled. Since BCWS and BCWP will always be equal at the end of the project, the SV is always zero at the end of the project.	Accomplishment variance
CV = BCWP – ACWP (CV = EV – AC)	Cost variance (CV) indicates that the actual cost to complete some amount of work was different from the originally budgeted. A positive CV indicates that the work was done for less than the budgeted amount. A negative CV indicates that the work cost more to complete than originally budgeted.	Cost variance
VaC = BaC EaC	Variance at completion (VaC) indicates that the estimated cost at completion will be different from the originally budgeted. A positive VaC forecasts a project underrun. A negative VaC forecasts a project overrun.	Forecast overrun or underrun

TABLE 4.7

Performance Information for Two Projects

		Project 1		Project 2	
Month	PV	EV1	AC1	EV2	AC2
1	$100	$100	$100	$75	$50
2	$200	$175	$200	$150	$125
3	$250	$225	$300	$250	$225
4	$300	$275	$400	$325	$325
5	$450	$400	$500	$475	$450
6	$550	$475	$625	$600	$575
7	$650				
8	$800				
9	$900				
10	$1000				
BaC	$1000				

a simple linear approach. In Table 4.7, the third and fourth columns show the EV and actual cost (AC) for project 1 for the first six months, and the fifth and sixth columns show the EV and AC for project 2. Remember, the EV is based on the budgeted cost of the work that is actually completed. For example, after two months, project 1 has an EV of $175. So, even though project 1 was scheduled to get $200 worth of work completed by the end of the second month, project 1 only completed $175 worth of work. However, the true cost of that work was $200. In traditional PERT/CPM, the actual cost of $200 would be compared to the planned cost of $200, and the conclusion would be that the project is on budget. In reality, the project is slightly over budget because it cost $200 to complete only $175 worth of work. Figures 4.12 and 4.13 show the EV information from Table 4.7 in a graphical chart for each project.

Figure 4.14 displays the calculation of the schedule variance (SV) and the schedule performance index (SPI), two common representations of schedule performance. Notice that the SV and SPI make use of the same variables in their calculations: EV and PV. However, the SV utilizes the difference between these two variables, and the SPI uses the ratio of these two variables.

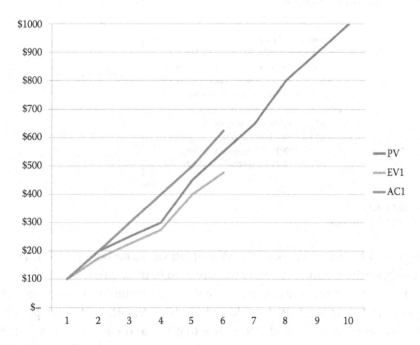

FIGURE 4.12
EV information for project 1.

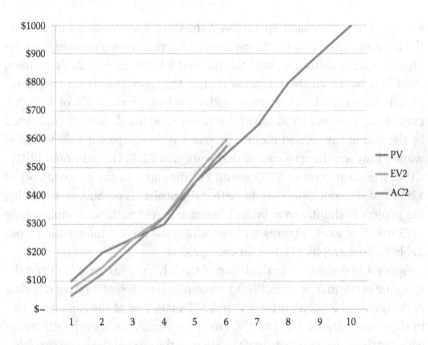

FIGURE 4.13
EV information for project 2.

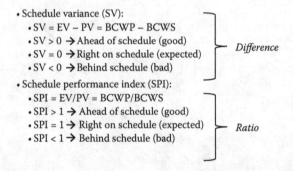

FIGURE 4.14
SV and SPI metrics.

Figures 4.15 and 4.16 present the SV and SPI values for both projects. Table 4.8 shows the SV and SPI values that are used in these charts.

Figure 4.17 shows the calculation of the cost variance (CV) and the cost performance index (CPI), two common representations of cost performance. Similar to SV and SPI, notice that CV and CPI make use of the same variables in their calculations: EV and AC. However, CV utilizes the difference between these two variables, and CPI uses the ratio of these two

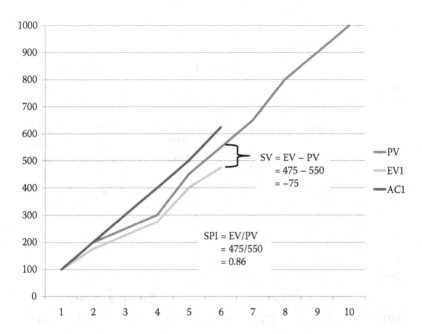

FIGURE 4.15
SV and SPI metrics for project 1.

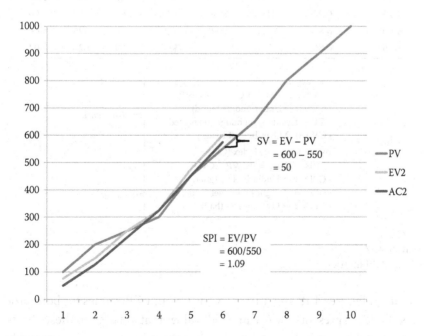

FIGURE 4.16
SV and SPI metrics for project 2.

TABLE 4.8

Summary of EV Metrics

		Project 1		Project 2	
Month	PV	EV1	AC1	EV2	AC2
1	$100	$100	$100	$75	$50
2	$200	$175	$200	$150	$125
3	$250	$225	$300	$250	$225
4	$300	$275	$400	$325	$325
5	$450	$400	$500	$475	$450
6	$550	$475	$625	$600	$575
7	$650				
8	$800				
9	$900				
10	$1000				
BaC	$1000				

Project 1 EV Metrics				Project 2 EV Metrics			
SV1	SPI1	CV1	CPI1	SV2	SPI2	CV2	CPI2
–	1.00	–	1.00	$(25)	0.75	$25	1.50
$(25)	0.88	$(25)	0.88	$(50)	0.75	$25	1.20
$(25)	0.90	$(75)	0.75	–	1.00	$25	1.11
$(25)	0.92	$(125)	0.69	$25	1.08	–	1.00
$(50)	0.89	$(100)	0.80	$25	1.06	$25	1.06
$(75)	0.86	$(150)	0.76	$50	1.09	$25	1.04

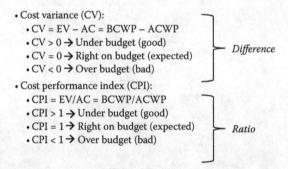

- Cost variance (CV):
  - CV = EV – AC = BCWP – ACWP ⎤
  - CV > 0 → Under budget (good) ⎟
  - CV = 0 → Right on budget (expected) ⎬ *Difference*
  - CV < 0 → Over budget (bad) ⎟
- Cost performance index (CPI):
  - CPI = EV/AC = BCWP/ACWP ⎤
  - CPI > 1 → Under budget (good) ⎟
  - CPI = 1 → Right on budget (expected) ⎬ *Ratio*
  - CPI < 1 → Over budget (bad) ⎦

FIGURE 4.17
CV and CPI metrics.

variables. Figures 4.18 and 4.19 show the CV and CPI values for both projects. Table 4.8 presents the CV and CPI values that are used in these charts.

As stated earlier in this section, EV has some limitations. For example, there is no indication of a *critical path*. So, while EV shows performance

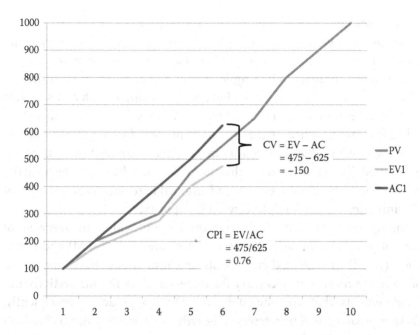

FIGURE 4.18
CV and CPI metrics for project 1.

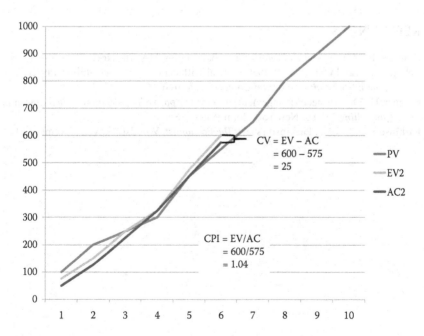

FIGURE 4.19
CV and CPI metrics for project 2.

data, it does not give any indication of the interconnection of tasks. There is also no indication of the quality (or appropriateness) of the work being accomplished. Third, EV is not well suited to some of the newer project management approaches like Agile project management or even simpler structures such as level of effort. Finally, the *dollarized* value of schedule performance does not fully capture time. As a result, another calculation called the earned schedule (ES) has been proposed to use in conjunction with the cost variables for EV that make a better connection to time. ES will not be discussed as part of this book because it has yet to be formally accepted into the EVM arena. It is mentioned here only as an example of the limitations of the straightforward EV approach.

Throughout this chapter, the authors have provided an overview of current popular approaches to project planning (PERT/CPM) and evaluation (EVM) as well as their benefits and limitations. Basic knowledge of these approaches is necessary for understanding the innovations and improvements that are offered by the DPM approach. Consequently, these approaches will be referenced heavily in Chapters 5, 6, and 8, which describe the DPM.

REFERENCES

Goldratt, E. M. 1997. *Critical Chain*. Great Barrington, MA: The North River Press.
Kelley, Jr., J. E. and Walker, M. R. 1959. Critical-Path Planning and Scheduling. *Proceedings of the Eastern Joint Computer Conference*, March.
Kerzner, H. 2001. Project Management: *A Systems Approach to Planning, Scheduling, and Controlling*, 7th ed. New York: John Wiley & Sons.
Parkinson, C. N. 1955. Parkinson's law. *The Economist,* Woodstock, VA, November 19.

5

The New Approach of Dynamic Progress Method

INTRODUCTION

As stated in Chapter 4, there are three major flaws with the traditional program evaluation and review technique (PERT)/critical path method (CPM) project planning technique:

1. Task duration is an input.
2. Resource productivity impacts are not considered.
3. Management corrective actions are not captured.

The Dynamic Progress Method (DPM) aims to remove these flaws from project planning because they are big contributors to the mismanagement of many projects. One of the biggest risks in project management is to start with an unrealistic (and perhaps unachievable) baseline project plan. When the baseline plan is published, many activities and commitments are set in motion within the prime contractor company and the subcontractor companies. Once committed to, these decisions and resulting resource allocations are sometimes difficult to change quickly. This delay between recognizing the need to change the commitments of resources and actually implementing the change in allocation of resources can easily be weeks long in most companies and even months long in some companies. This causes any project performance issues to worsen during this delay period, which only takes the project further off its intended track. Thus, one of the first goals of the DPM is to establish a more realistic baseline plan for a given project so that the expectations (and subsequent commitments) are reasonable and achievable. It is much better to know *bad news* upfront than to cruise along with our metaphorical heads in the sand like an ostrich and *hope* to somehow get lucky and meet the performance goals for the project. Hope is not a strategy, and ostrich management kills organizations.

To address the three major flaws of the PERT/CPM, at a minimum, the DPM has to incorporate the following:

- A task-level operational simulation model that incorporates resources performing work
- Management corrective actions based on task and/or project performance status (i.e., behind schedule, over budget)
- Real-world negative impacts on work throughput (e.g., productivity) of applying these management corrective actions (e.g., productivity losses based on the accumulation of fatigue when working overtime and overmanning when allocating additional resources to a task beyond the *planned* amount)

There are additional elements that can be incorporated, such as the removal of tasks from the project because the overall scope of the project is reduced to help it get back on track. However, these are very advanced concepts and require a great deal of additional model structure to accomplish. The purpose of this book is to introduce the DPM (resource-based approach) as an alternative approach to the traditional PERT/CPM (duration-based approach) for project planning and management. It is fully expected that the definition of the DPM, as well as its content, will evolve over time beyond the publication of this book.

A SIMPLE PROJECT FRAMEWORK FOR CONSIDERATION

In an effort to understand how the DPM can be used on projects, it is important to first understand the overall framework within which we are working. For any project, there is a combination of things that occur. It begins with the work breakdown structure (WBS), which is the list of activities and work tasks that must be completed, along with the necessary dependencies among these activities and tasks, to accomplish the project. (*Note*: The WBS goes by many names, but for the purposes of this book, we will use the generic term WBS to describe the list of tasks and their dependencies.) Next, resources (e.g., people, equipment, materials) are applied to do this work. In the end, work is accomplished through the application of these resources, and a final schedule of completed tasks and a final cost of the entire project can be documented. This framework, along with arrows indicating the direction of cause and effect, is captured in Figure 5.1. In this figure, we see the WBS and available resources come together to give us the final schedule and final cost for the project.

The diagram in Figure 5.1 is not yet complete. In the real world, as the work on a project progresses, slight changes and corrections are made along the way if the project gets off track. For example, if the project appears to be progressing slower than expected (to the point that it can be considered behind schedule or late), the project manager may decide to increase the resources that are assigned to key tasks in an attempt to speed up progress. Or, he or she may decide to work the resources overtime to get more work done to increase progress. These are corrections that are made by the project manager, and they are the result of management policies. Management policies, also called management actions, are the feedback mechanisms that control the project and determine what actions a project manager can take to improve project performance. For example, a management policy may state that no overtime is allowed or may state that a limit of 4 h/day of overtime is allowed. Or, there may even be a more complex management policy that allows for a little bit of overtime when a project is a little bit behind schedule (e.g., 1 h/day) but allows for a lot of overtime if the project is very far behind schedule (e.g., 8 h/day). The point here is that no project operates in a vacuum. Project managers and team members are always making slight adjustments to the original assignments to keep the project on track. For instance, a critical material required for the project may be delivered late from the supplier, which

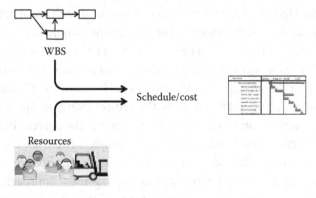

FIGURE 5.1
Combination of WBS and resources to accomplish a project.

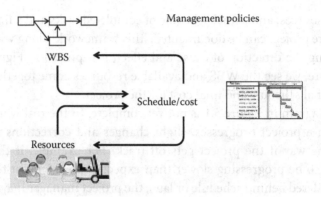

FIGURE 5.2
Management policies as feedback mechanisms for project control.

causes the project to now be behind schedule. This may not be a fault of the company doing the work, but it is now a disruption in the progress of the project that must be accounted for, and adjustments to how and when resources are used, must occur to correct project performance so that the project can finish within the acceptable schedule and cost parameters. Figure 5.2 captures the role of management policies in the overall project. The objective of management policies is to assess the state of the project with respect to the desired final schedule and cost goals and then to make changes to the WBS (e.g., remove a noncritical task from the project or shift two tasks to work in parallel) and the allocation of resources (e.g., add more resources, work overtime) to shift project performance back toward the desired final schedule and cost goals.

The problem with current PERT/CPM planning and management approaches is that they do not include elements of the full framework that is shown in Figure 5.2, as mentioned in Chapter 4 with the discussion of earned value. Although resource considerations may have been used to make the initial project estimates, once the plan is developed, resources are typically no longer considered. This creates a disconnect between the resources and the project schedule and cost. However, we all know that it takes resources to do work and move the project along, so this disconnection is a disconnection from reality. Furthermore, the current PERT/CPM approaches offer a single static view of the project. There are no feedback mechanisms that are included. Figure 5.3 shows the limited approach that is embodied in the current planning and management approaches. Using PERT/CPM tools, it is impossible to understand if particular management policies or corrective actions will help the project because management

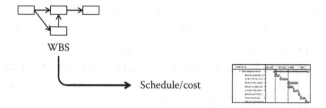

FIGURE 5.3
PERT/CPM approaches lack consideration for resources and management policies.

corrective actions are not a formal part of the PERT/CPM framework, and resources are not considered on an ongoing basis. As seen in Figure 5.3, the PERT/CPM provides an overly simplistic view of the project. This oversimplification introduces a huge amount of risk.

DPM AND PERT/CPM: DIFFERENT SIDES OF THE SAME COIN

This section will begin to lay the groundwork for the DPM so that similarities and differences with the PERT/CPM can be highlighted throughout the rest of the book. In addition, this section lays out some basic concepts for the DPM that will be built upon and expanded in later chapters.

In many situations, the DPM and the PERT/CPM provide different schedule and cost estimates for the same project. However, in theory, the DPM and the PERT/CPM should provide the *exact same estimates*. Figure 5.4 shows the basic thought process an experienced project manager may go through when estimating a task for a project. He or she may know roughly how much work needs to be done, who is probably going to do it, how *good* that person (or group of people) is, and the general availability of that person (or group of people). All this information filters through to generate an expected duration for the task. In Figure 5.4, some values are provided

Expected amount of work	×		×	Assumed productivity level	×	Assumed availability (days, h/day)	=	Expected duration
(80 h)		Joe (1)		(100%)		(8 h/day)		(10 days)

FIGURE 5.4
Project manager assumptions.

to make this connection. The project manager knows that there is a bucket of work to do (about 80 h of work) and that Joe will most likely be the person doing the work (1 person). The project manager knows that Joe is one of the more productive employees (e.g., productivity of 100%), and Joe works a typical day at the office, which is 8 h/day. Given that information, the task should take 10 days to finish.

$$\text{Duration} = (\text{work to do})/(\text{completion rate})$$

$$= 80 \text{ h}/(1 \text{ person} \times 100\% \text{ productivity} \times 8 \text{ h/person/day})$$

$$= 80 \text{ h}/(8 \text{ h/day})$$

$$= 10 \text{ days}.$$

(*Note*: Although this explanation may not be exactly correct for every project manager, it is roughly correct. The project manager [or whoever is providing the estimate] *somehow* looks at the amount of work to do and compares it against the rate at which that work can be accomplished. If he or she [or whoever is providing the estimate] *does not* do this and simply states a duration with no thought process supporting it, this will obviously lead to trouble, so we will not even consider that situation. The random assignment of a duration to a task is one of the minor issues with user-friendly PERT/CPM tools that was stated at the "Additional Issues with PERT/CPM" section in Chapter 4. Clearly, no matter what tool is used, a thoughtless estimating approach will yield poor results, so let us spend our time looking at the techniques that are used by well-intentioned project managers who are getting poor project performance as a result of the tool that they are using and not their own thought processes.)

Once the project manager has this information, a PERT/CPM tool uses the task duration as an input (Figure 5.5, right side). If any resource information is also input into the PERT/CPM tool by the project manager, it is not used to generate the initial duration. This initial duration is a *direct input* from the project manager into the tool, that is, he or she actually types this number into the tool. As stated in Chapter 4 as one of the major flaws of the PERT/CPM, in the real world, duration is an *output*, not an *input*. On the other hand, the DPM uses the resource information as inputs (Figure 5.5, left side). Notice that if all things were perfect, and the resource assumptions proved to be true in real life, the DPM and the PERT/CPM would both provide the exact same duration for the task

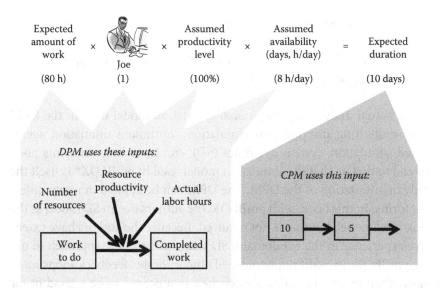

FIGURE 5.5
PERT/CPM uses task duration as an input.

(10 days). By using resource-based inputs, the DPM can more realistically capture the differences that occur in the real world and the consequences on project performance of these differences. For instance, suppose that Joe is a senior-level programmer with 20 years of experience, and he is replaced by Pete, a programmer who is fresh out of college, because Joe is committed to a higher-priority project. Most likely, Pete would not perform at the same level of *productivity* as Joe. As a result, this simple substitution of a resource could cause the project to become very late, even if no other changes were made to the project plan. In the PERT/CPM, the disconnection of duration from the resources misses these types of real-world differences that can have major impacts on project performance.

DPM AND SYSTEM DYNAMICS

As stated at the beginning of this chapter, the DPM incorporates the following:

- A task-level operational simulation model that incorporates resources performing work

- Management corrective actions based on task and/or project performance status
- Real-world negative impacts on work throughput of applying these management corrective actions

The actual underlying operational simulation model used in the DPM can be anything: discrete event simulation, continuous simulation, agent-based simulation, system dynamics (SD), etc. In no way does this book intend to dictate that the simulation model used in pmBLOX® is itself the only manifestation of the DPM. The DPM can be applied in many different forms. In this book, with pmBLOX, the authors use an SD model as the task-level model, but that is not required. Because the authors have extensive experience in the SD domain, SD was chosen as the approach to use for pmBLOX. In addition, because SD incorporates feedback loops more easily than other simulation approaches, it appeared to be a good fit for incorporating management policies and management corrective actions (which are feedback mechanisms).

For the authors, the origins of the DPM come from earlier applications of SD to project planning and project management. The *System Dynamics Review*, a journal published quarterly by the System Dynamics Society, recently released a virtual edition in the first quarter of 2013 that focused on the application of SD to project management. Some of the references recorded in this virtual edition are listed at the end of this chapter.

(*Note*: The rest of this section will delve into some of the model details that will be more adequately explained in Chapter 6.)

In summary, most of the project-related work conducted in the SD field has focused at the *strategic management* level (i.e., project level, such that the major thing to be studied is the entire project as a whole). With these types of studies, a single simulation model is developed for an entire project with *work units* or *tasks* flowing through the model. Again, the focus is the whole project. A commonly cited example of this type of strategic-level model can be seen in Figure 5.6. This book will not go into the details of this model. Instead, this model serves as an example of the current state of project management applications in the SD domain so that the DPM details in this chapter and Chapter 6 can be compared where necessary. The Readers are encouraged to look at the reference sources for this strategic-level model and the other SD example models that are found at the end of this chapter for additional information and details.

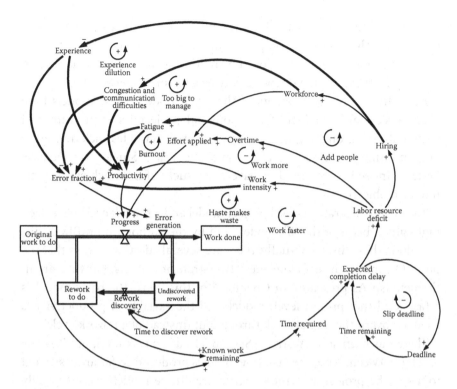

FIGURE 5.6
Strategic-level SD model for project planning. (From Lyneis, J. M. and D. N. Ford, *System Dynamics Review* 23: 157–189, used with permission of publisher, 2007.)

The strategic-level SD model used in Figure 5.6 also utilizes the concept of rework in relation to work that is accomplished. Figure 5.7 portrays this concept more clearly. Sometimes, work that is *accomplished* is not actually *complete*. There may be mistakes with the work. Through some quality assurance or review process, these mistakes are found and must

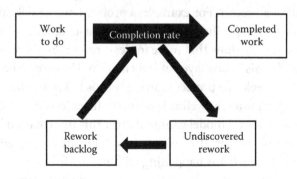

FIGURE 5.7
Discovery and completion of rework.

be *reworked* to make the final deliverable match the quality level that is expected. Only then, after completion of the rework, can the work be considered complete. Depending on the abilities of the resources applied to the project, this additional rework may be a lot, or it may be a little.

According to the proponents of these SD models, these models have been successful with identifying potential project issues upfront and with addressing ongoing project issues. Noted examples include Ingalls Shipbuilding, Fluor Corporation, and the Peace Shield Air Defense System. Indeed, these models have been successful in achieving their intended objectives.

The ideas of a strategic-level project model and a rework cycle have been highlighted because the SD model used by the authors in pmBLOX differs along these lines. (Actually, there are several additional ways that the pmBLOX model differs from these two strategic models, but they are in the details.) As presented in Chapter 6 of this book, the basic model is a task-level (not project-level) model, and the variable of productivity is used to govern the rate of work throughput (instead of a rework cycle).

There has been some work on SD models at the task level, but it is few and far between. And, the task-level models produced so far are restricted to a specific project size and/or structure. These models were typically developed as a consulting engagement on a specific project. Thus, their usage is limited because the tools are not widely available for others to use (i.e., the tools are proprietary to the consulting organizations), are not capable of handling large (or even medium-sized) projects, or are not flexible enough to model different situations (i.e., the tools have a strict model structure that is designed for a specific type of analysis).

The authors use a task-level model to mimic real-world activities and create a tool that can be used operationally to guide the planning and management of a project. For example, a project-level model cannot show which tasks a set of specific resources should be assigned to. The project-level model can only show that more (or less) resources are required at an aggregate level. This is one layer of information. However, to manage the project week to week, the project manager needs to know which resources are going to which tasks, as well as how these allocations may change along the way. A project-level model cannot deliver this information because its granularity is insufficient. If a task is not specifically simulated, then it is impossible to know what is happening with it.

With regards to rework, the authors use a productivity variable to capture work throughput capabilities. Both rework and productivity are equivalent methods. The point is that sometimes, it takes longer to do a certain amount of work. For instance, it may take 8 h to do 6-h worth of assigned work because the employee takes bathroom breaks, talks in the hallway, makes mistakes and has to fix them, etc. The rework cycle accomplishes this by making a set of work go through the process multiple times before it is complete. The productivity variable slows work down so that it goes through the process more slowly (but every piece of work that goes through is considered *complete*). As a simple example, consider a task (or project) with 8 h of *work to do*. If all of this work had to be reworked, it would take 16 h to finish the original *8 h* of work. Using productivity, the equivalent is to say that productivity is 50%, that is, for every hour worked, only a half-hour of *true* work was completed. Both of these approaches yield 8 h of true work while paying for 16 h of resource time.

One of the main reasons that the authors use a productivity variable instead of a rework cycle is that the rework cycle itself has some mechanical issues when running a simulation. If the rework rate is set to 10%, for example, then each time work is done, 10% of the work has to be done again. This is a never-ending loop: 10% of 10% of 10% and so on. With this approach, the work would never be completely finished. To eliminate this endless loop, the programmer of the rework cycle model sets a limit to the number of rework loops (say, three rework loops) or some minimal amount of work (say, the remaining 1% of work to do) at which the work is considered complete. Thus, the rework cycle model is not used in its entirety; it is short-circuited. At that point, why bother with a rework loop? The authors feel that a productivity variable represents a cleaner and more straightforward method for capturing the same dynamic.

Note: The models with rework cycles sometimes also include a productivity variable, but the issue still remains that an endless loop of rework has to be stopped at some point.

With this overview of the DPM, we can now look back at the three flaws of the PERT/CPM that were mentioned at the beginning of this chapter:

1. Task duration is an input.
2. Resource productivity impacts are not considered.
3. Management corrective actions are not captured.

Details of the pmBLOX DPM model will be shown in Chapter 6, but at this point, it can already be seen that the DPM approach described in this book addresses the three flaws because (1) it simulates the use of resources accomplishing work at the task level, (2) it incorporates productivity considerations for resources, and (3) it employs management corrective actions along with their productivity consequences.

REFERENCES*

Abdel-Hamid, T. K. 1989. The dynamics of software project staffing: A system dynamics based simulation approach. *IEEE Transactions on Software Engineering* 15 (2): 109–119.

Abdel-Hamid, T. K. and S. E. Madnick. 1991. *Software Project Dynamics: An Integrated Approach*. Englewood Cliffs, NJ: Prentice-Hall.

Cooper, K. G. 1980. Naval ship production: A claim settled and a framework built. *Interfaces* 10 (6): 20–36.

Cooper, K. G. 1996. System dynamics methods in complex project management. In T. M. Williams (Ed.), *Managing and Modeling Complex Projects*. In *Proceedings of the NATO Advanced Research Workshop on Managing and Modeling Complex Projects*, Kiev, Ukraine, Nov. 13–15, published in *NATO ASI Series 4. Science and Technology Policy*, Vol. 17.

Ford, D. N. and J. D. Sterman. 1998. Dynamic modeling of product development processes. *System Dynamics Review* 14 (1): 31–68.

Godlewski, E., G. Lee, and K. Cooper. 2012. System dynamics transforms fluor project and change management. *Interfaces* 42 (1): 17–32.

Graham, A. K. 2000. Beyond PM101: Lessons for managing large development programs. *Project Management Journal* 31 (4): 7–18.

Howick, S. 2003. Using system dynamics to analyse disruption and delay in complex projects for litigation: Can the modeling purposes be met? *Journal of Operational Research Society* 54: 222–229.

Lee, Z., D. Ford, and N. Joglekar. 2007. Resource allocation policy design for reduced project duration: A systems modeling approach. *Systems Research and Behavioral Science* 24: 1–15.

Lyneis, J. M. and D. N. Ford. 2007. System dynamics applied to project management: A survey, assessment, and directions for future research. *System Dynamics Review* 23 (4): 157–189.

Lyneis, J. M., K. G. Cooper, and S. A. Els. 2001. Strategic management of complex projects: A case study using system dynamics. *System Dynamics Review* 17 (3): 237–260.

Rahmandad, H. and D. Weiss. 2009. Dynamics of concurrent software development. *System Dynamics Review* 25 (3): 224–249.

Repenning, N. P. 2000. A dynamic model of resource allocation in multi-project research and development systems. *System Dynamics Review* 16 (3): 173–212.

Rodrigues, A. G. and J. Bowers. 1996. The role of system dynamics in project management. *International Journal of Project Management* 14 (4): 213–220.

Sterman, J. D. 2000. *Business Dynamics: Systems Thinking and Modeling for a Complex World*. Chicago, IL: Irwin/McGraw Hill.

---

* The following list of references provides the readers with more details of the SD project models that are mentioned in this chapter.

6

Overview of the Dynamic Progress
Method Simulation Model

INTRODUCTION

The simulation model used on the Defense Advanced Research Project Agency (DARPA) research project and in pmBLOX® will be explained in this chapter. The simulation model will be built up section by section to help the readers fully understand all the elements of the model and why they are important. Examples will be provided throughout the chapter. In the figures in this chapter, the black elements represent variables and interconnections that exist in most traditional project management (PM) tools. The light-gray elements are additional elements that are part of the DPM approach.

BASIC TASK STRUCTURE

In the task simulation model used in pmBLOX (the DPM-based software included with this book), resources and work activities are captured in an operational model (i.e., a model of the operations or activities that actually occur). This begins with the representation of task work. As seen in Figure 6.1, there are two buckets of work: work to do and completed work. Work to do represents all the work that is associated with the task prior to applying any resources to the task (i.e., the task work backlog). Completed work represents all the work that is accomplished on the task by applying resources to do work on the task. Before a task is initiated, the work-to-do stock is full, and the completed-work stock is empty. When the task is

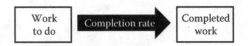

FIGURE 6.1
Basic task model with work to do and completed work.

complete, the work-to-do stock is empty, and the completed-work stock is full.

The mechanism that moves work from work to do to completed work is the completion rate. The completion rate is equal to the *effective* labor hours, which are the product of the number of resources and the actual labor hours that were worked on that day (Figure 6.2). For example, if there are two people who are assigned to the task, and they both work 8 h on a given day, the *completion rate* would be (2 persons × 8 h/person) = 16 h of work. If only one person works for 8 h on that same task, the completion rate would only be 8 h of work. Given this basic approach, if the completion rate remained constant for all days, it would be easy to calculate the expected duration of the task. For instance, if a task has 80 h of work to do with a constant completion rate of 8 h/day (due to one person working 8 h each day), the expected duration of that task is 10 days:

Task duration
= Work to do ÷ completion rate
= 80 h ÷ (8 h/day)
= 10 days.

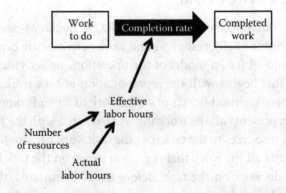

FIGURE 6.2
Basic task model with *effective labor hours*.

If a project manager is accustomed to using durations as inputs for tasks (as with the CPM approach), he or she may look at this approach and question how someone would even be able to guess the amount of work hours that are required for a task (i.e., work to do). However, every PM tool currently on the market does this calculation behind the scenes, whether the users know it or not. For instance, suppose that we used a typical duration-based CPM tool and input 10 days as the duration of this task. As soon as we assign one person to that task, the traditional PM tool will back-calculate the work hours for the task. The formula is the same as above:

Task duration
= Work to do ÷ completion rate.

Now, however, the task duration and completion rate are known:

Work to do
= Task duration × completion rate
= 10 days × (8 h/day)
= 80 h.

We can test this in a traditional PM tool by changing the number of resources that are assigned to the task. If the reader were to change the number of resources to two people or change the level of effort from 100% to 200% (to represent twice as many people), the task duration would immediately change to 5 days:

Task duration
= Work to do ÷ completion rate
= 80 h ÷ (16 h/day)
= 5 days.

This is essentially what typical CPM-based tools will do when they are in *effort-driven* mode. This is also how traditional PM tools can cause problems. If we were to change the number of resources from 1 to 10, the duration of the task would be reduced to 10% of the original duration. The traditional PM tools assume a linear relationship between the number of people who are assigned to a task and their work rate. More often than not, this is a bad assumption. A typical analogy that is used in this case is to say

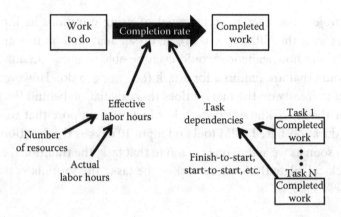

FIGURE 6.3
Basic task model with task dependencies.

that it is like nine women having a baby in one month. For some tasks, this is impossible. (This issue will be addressed by the DPM approach with the discussion of Figure 6.16.)

Figure 6.3 adds the constraints on the progress of a task that is based on dependencies with other tasks on a project (e.g., finish-to-start dependency, as described in Chapter 4 with the CPM). There may be a limit to the amount of work that can be done on a task due to a dependency on the amount of completed work for a separate task. Even if resources are available to work on our current task, the completion rate would be set to zero until the dependency constraint is satisfied. (More details will be provided in Chapter 7 on how to set these dependencies in pmBLOX.)

At any point, the schedule and cost status of the task can be obtained (Figure 6.4). On most government agency projects and some commercial projects, earned value (EV) is used to determine the schedule and cost status of a task or project. But, other PM tools may use different metrics to determine where a task stands in relation to the scheduled end date of the task and the budgeted total cost of the task. pmBLOX uses EV metrics, specifically the schedule performance index (SPI), to denote *schedule pressure* and the cost performance index (CPI) to represent *cost pressure* because these are formally accepted standard metrics that are used by many in the PM field.

As a quick refresher, the basic formula for SPI is the following:

SPI
= EV ÷ planned value.

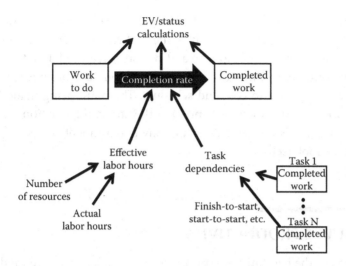

FIGURE 6.4
Basic task model with status calculations.

Sometimes, this is also written as the following:

SPI
= Budgeted cost of work performed (BCWP) ÷ budgeted cost of work
  scheduled (BCWS).

If the SPI < 1, the task (or project) is considered behind schedule. If
the SPI = 1, the task (or project) is considered exactly on schedule. If the
SPI > 1, the task (or project) is considered ahead of schedule.

Similarly, the basic formulas for CPI are the following:

CPI
= EV ÷ actual cost
CPI
= BCWP ÷ actual cost of work performed (ACWP)

If the CPI < 1, the task (or project) is considered over budget. If the
CPI = 1, the task (or project) is considered exactly on budget. If the CPI > 1,
the task (or project) is considered under budget.

(More details will be provided in Chapter 7 on how EV metrics are used
in pmBLOX.)

The limitation with traditional PM tools is that they only provide this status information. Unfortunately, some of them do not even provide this type of status information, and an add-on tool is required. But, for now, let us assume that all traditional CPM-based PM tools can provide task status information relative to cost and schedule. The point being made here is that traditional PM tools only provide the status information. This status information is not used as part of any management corrective action within the tool itself.

RESOURCE PRODUCTIVITY

As stated at the beginning of this chapter, the elements of the model that are shown in black in Figure 6.4 are elements that exist in most traditional PM tools. We will now discuss the additional elements that are added to the model for the DPM. Figure 6.5 shows the addition of a variable called resource productivity in the calculation of the effective labor hours. Resource productivity is simply a way to capture the different work rates of resources, and it can be defined in several ways.

With the first method, resource productivity is a measure of the proportion of *productive* time that a resource spends on a task, where productive

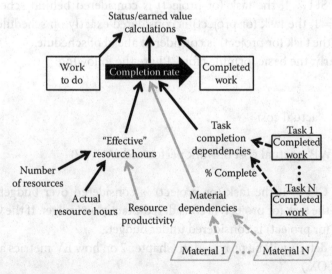

FIGURE 6.5
Basic task model with resource productivity.

time is the time that is applied against the work to do for the task. For example, a person may be at the office for 8 h during a day (and, therefore, getting paid by the project for 8 h), but he or she may only get 6 h of actual task work done during the day due to other meetings, chatting at the water cooler, taking a cigarette break, going to the bathroom, staying out for a long lunch, etc. In this case, his or her productivity is 75% (6 h of work/8 h at the office = 0.75).

With the second method, resource productivity can also be used to differentiate the work rates among different resources. For example, a junior-level engineer or software developer typically has a lower level of proficiency and effectiveness (i.e., productivity) than a senior-level engineer or software developer. In this case, if a senior-level engineer is 100% productive, a junior-level engineer may be only 50% productive, which indicates that it would take the latter twice as long to accomplish the same task as the former. Or, if we use the junior engineer as the baseline and say that he or she is 100% productive, in this case, the senior engineer may have a productivity level of 200% (gets twice the work done in the same amount of time).

Resource productivity is part of the product of variables that results in effective labor hours as follows:

Effective labor hours
= Number of resources × actual labor hours × resource productivity.

Using the example of the junior- and senior-level engineers, we might have the following:

Effective labor hours for senior engineer
= 1 person × 8 h/day/person × 100%
= 8 h for the completion rate

Effective labor hours for junior engineer
= 1 person × 8 h/day/person × 50%
= 4 h for the completion rate.

If a task has 80 h of work to do, it would take the senior engineer 10 days to finish the task working 8 h/day (80 h ÷ [8 h/day] = 10 days). The junior engineer would take 20 days to finish the same task working 8 h/day

(80 h ÷ [4 h/day] = 20 days). Thus, simply changing resources for a task can often have significant impacts on the duration of the task, even if all the tasks stay the exact same.

While the addition of the resource productivity variable seems quite simple, traditional PM tools make it difficult to capture this. Often, when a resource on the project changes, the project manager simply changes the name of the resource in the plan and keeps everything the same. Consequently, the project plan is shown to be the same. In reality, this is usually not the case. Having worked previously at large companies, the authors have seen this phenomenon firsthand. During the proposal phase, we might develop a project plan with the assumption that we would have some of the *best* people available to work on the project because we wanted to show the customers that we could do a lot of work in a short period of time (and, thus, provide high value to the potential customers). The assumption of using the best people results in an aggressive work schedule. Nine months later, when the contract is actually awarded, the resources that we assumed would work on the project may no longer be available. Instead, we often have to use people who are new to the organization. Or, worse, we have to utilize people who have not been selected by other project teams and are metaphorically at the *bottom of the barrel*. In these cases, most of the time, we still use the same work schedule because it is now contractually mandated. By changing resources, we inadvertently change the productivity rate of the work being done, which ultimately affects the duration of the project. Unfortunately, it usually takes a couple of weeks or even months and a significant schedule slip to figure this out.

It should be noted that traditional PM tools *can* incorporate the concept of resource productivity, but the methods are often circuitous and cumbersome. For instance, suppose that we want to indicate that a resource has a productivity level of 75%. Because the traditional PM tool assumes that paid time is equivalent to task work time, we could change the number of hours that the person works in a day from 8 h/day to 6 h/day. This would ensure that the amount of work done each day is correct. But, we would then need to change the hourly pay rate for this resource from, say, $20/h (or $160/day) to $26.67/h (to match the same $160/day with just 6 h). Using these methods, the work rate and cost are now correct. However, when someone else looks at the plan and sees that the resource is just working 6 h/day, that someone may question that. And, any EV calculations may now be affected. As a project manager, it is also easy to forget that all these changes have been made and where exactly they have been made. Thus, when it is time to pass the project plan along to someone else or publish the plan for others to see, it is easy to accidentally pass along or show a plan that looks suspicious because the resource values have not been *reverted back* to the actual numbers. In essence, while these types of productivity considerations can be accommodated in traditional PM tools, the *gaming* that is required can sometimes cause more problems.

As shown in Figure 6.5 in this chapter, resource productivity acts as a multiplier on the actual labor hours in the equation for effective labor hours. By default, pmBLOX assumes a resource productivity of 100% (i.e., multiplier of 1.0) until this is changed by the user. By not including productivity as a direct input, traditional PM tools also assume a productivity rate of 100%.

Note: In addition to resource productivity, Figure 6.5 also makes some other changes relative to Figure 6.4 that will be used moving forward. Figure 6.5 splits the task dependencies into task completion dependencies and material dependencies because pmBLOX allows both types of dependencies. For task completion dependencies, pmBLOX uses *percent complete* (% complete) instead of the CPM-based finish-to-start (FS), start-to-start (SS), etc. This input will be described in Chapter 7, section "Example 8—Task Dependencies." For material dependencies, see Chapter 7, section "Example 9—Working with Materials."

MANAGEMENT CORRECTIVE ACTIONS

Figure 6.6 shows the next set of model parameters that are unique to the DPM: corrective actions. Corrective actions are those changes that are made to the execution of a project to *correct* or alter its performance in some desired direction. These actions are similar to adjusting the steering wheel when driving a car to remain within the boundaries of the traffic lane on the street. Notice in Figure 6.6 that corrective actions stem from the EV/status calculations. What this means is that, in the real world, project managers will take actions to change the status of the project (with respect to cost and schedule) if the current state of the project is undesirable. When a project manager uses a traditional PM tool to plan or estimate a project, he or she gets a single, static, snapshot view of the project. No matter what happens, the plan shown in a traditional PM tool will

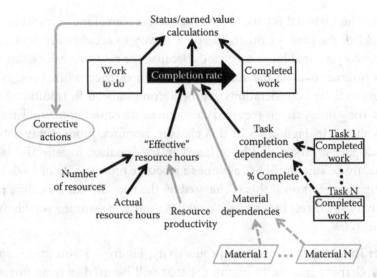

FIGURE 6.6
Basic task model with corrective actions.

not change. However, in the real world, project status information (e.g., EV metrics) often causes a project manager to react and actually make changes to the project. For example, if the allocated costs for a task are accumulated, and it appears to be over budget, in the real world, the project manager would make changes to the task to reduce cost to get the task back to the budgeted amount, such as reducing the labor resource that is applied to the task or shifting to a less expensive labor resource. As another example, if a task appears to be behind schedule (i.e., late), in the real world, the project manager would make changes to the task to accelerate the schedule to get the task back on schedule, such as adding more people to the task or assigning overtime to the current resources.

There are many corrective actions that a project manager can take to change the course of a project. Table 6.1 lists some of the most common corrective actions and their purposes. Of course, a project manager can also take any combination of these actions together or use different actions at different times on the project.

Other than terminating the project or altering the scope of the project, the four main outcomes that result from management corrective actions are the following:

1. Accelerate the schedule to get a late project back on track
2. Slow down the schedule to get an early project back on track

3. Reduce costs to get an overbudget project back on track
4. Increase costs to get an underbudget project back on track

Within pmBLOX, the only corrective actions that are allowed are the first four that are listed in Table 6.1, which involve changing the number of resources and the actual labor hours (Figure 6.7). pmBLOX does not deal with project termination or changes in project scope. These are not consistent management actions and, therefore, are difficult to incorporate into a simulation model. They change based on the unique circumstances of the project. For low-priority projects, it may not be a big deal to change the project scope to reduce the amount of work that is done. An example of this might be an internal research and development project for a new product in which the project has the flexibility of changing the features and capabilities of the project to meet the established internal budget. For high-priority projects, a change in scope (or project termination) may not be an option at all. For instance, consider a key project for a major customer. Many times, a company may take a financial hit on the project and purposely lose money to make sure that the customer is happy and the company retains the customers and business in the future. However, altering manpower quantities and the hours worked are much more consistent policies that can apply across a wide range of project situations, especially when tied to EV metrics. Thus, pmBLOX incorporates these options.

TABLE 6.1

Management Corrective Actions

Corrective Action	Purpose	Desired Outcome
Add resources	Increase work accomplished	Accelerate schedule to get a late project back on track.
Remove resources	Decrease work accomplished or reduce cost	Slow down schedule, reduce costs.
Work overtime	Increase work accomplished	Accelerate schedule to get a late project back on track.
Reduce work hours	Decrease work accomplished or reduce cost	Slow down schedule, reduce costs.
Extend the end date	Reduce schedule pressure	Get a late project back on track.
Change project scope	Reduce schedule and/or cost pressure	Eliminate work activities to get a late project back on track.
Terminate project	Reduce schedule and/or cost pressure	The project will be late and/or over budget, so *cut your losses* now.

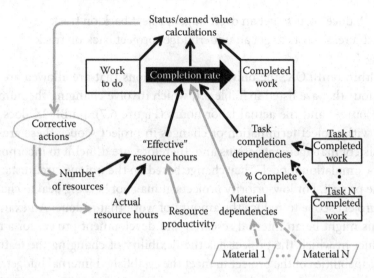

FIGURE 6.7
Basic task model with changes to resources and hours.

In the bulleted list above, notice that the first two management corrective action results are related to the schedule (i.e., duration) of a project or task, and the last two management corrective action results are associated to the cost of a project or task. Consider only the schedule-related results for now. The first result is to accelerate the project or task (i.e., reduce its duration), and the second result is to slow down the project or task (i.e., increase or lengthen its duration). Using the number of resources and actual labor hours, these two schedule-related results rely on an increase or decrease in the number of resources or an increase or decrease in the actual labor hours. Recall the equation for task duration from the "Basic Task Structure" section in this chapter:

Task duration = work to do ÷ completion rate.

Mathematically, the higher the completion rate, the lower the task duration (assuming that the work to do stays the same). As stated in the discussion about Table 6.1 earlier in this section, pmBLOX does not consider reductions in scope of work, so the work to do will, indeed, stay the same. Thus, if a task is behind schedule, and the project manager wants to accelerate the task (i.e., shorten its duration), the project manager needs to increase the completion rate (i.e., increase the effective labor hours):

Effective labor hours
= Number of resources × actual labor hours × resource productivity.

From the equation above, it can be seen that an increase in either the number of resources or the actual labor hours (or both) will cause an increase in the effective labor hours. (Assume that we are using the same resources so that the resource productivity remains constant.) Remember, all the corrective actions are driven by the current EV/status calculations, which are the SPI and the CPI. The former EV metric represents *schedule pressure*, and the latter EV metric represents *cost pressure*. pmBLOX allows the users to indicate how changes in SPI and CPI (i.e., task status) can lead to changes in the number of resources and actual labor hours (i.e., rate of work completion). pmBLOX uses a method called a *table function* to establish these relationships. We also sometimes call this relationship a management *policy*, which indicates a project manager's preferences for how he or she will manage a project under certain conditions.

Figure 6.8 provides an example of a table function describing the relationship between a change in SPI and a corresponding change in the actual labor hours that are assigned for a task. Specifically, Figure 6.8 shows how a decrease in SPI (i.e., the task is running late and falling behind schedule) leads to an increase in the number of overtime hours that are allocated to the assigned resources (which, in turn, increases the actual labor hours).

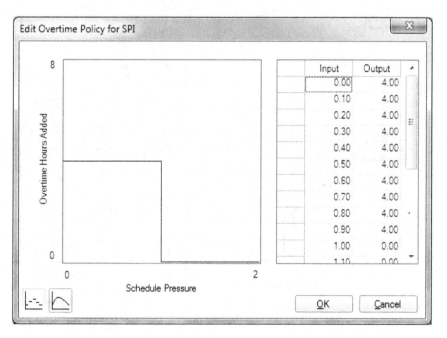

FIGURE 6.8
Aggressive overtime policy for SPI.

As the SPI decreases, and the task becomes later and later, the allocation of overtime increases in an attempt to get more work done to get the task back on schedule. For example, Figure 6.8 shows a very aggressive management policy that assigns 4 h of overtime as soon as the SPI drops below 1.0 (which indicates that the task is behind schedule). In Figure 6.8, the SPI is on the x-axis, and the number of overtime hours to assign to current resources on the task is on the y-axis. For every value of SPI that is below 1.0 (e.g., 0.90, 0.80), the corresponding number of overtime hours to assign is 4.

A less aggressive management policy might be to assign overtime hours in proportion to how late a task is (i.e., how low the SPI is) (Figure 6.9). When the task is only slightly behind schedule (e.g., SPI = 0.90), the project manager may only assign 1 h of overtime. When the task is moderately behind schedule (e.g., SPI = 0.70), the project manager may assign 2 h of overtime. And, when the project is severely behind schedule (e.g., SPI < 0.40), the project manager may assign 4 h of overtime. (More will be explained about the usage of management policies in Chapter 7.)

Similar to the management corrective action policies that add overtime hours to assigned resources when a task is behind schedule, another

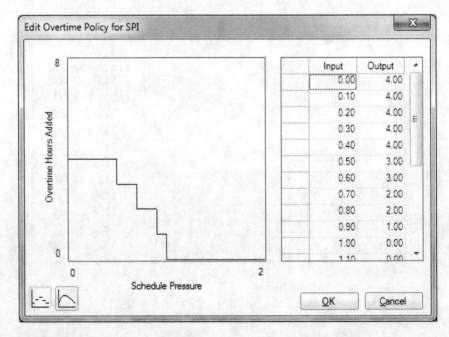

FIGURE 6.9
Proportional overtime policy for SPI.

corrective action is for a project manager to assign additional resources when a task is behind schedule. Figures 6.10 and 6.11 show examples of these table functions. In these table functions, the SPI is still on the x-axis, but now a multiplier on the number of resources is on the y-axis. For instance, Figure 6.10 shows an aggressive management policy that doubles the number of resources that are assigned to a task (i.e., multiplier = 2) as soon as the SPI falls below 1.0 (indicating that the task is late). Figure 6.11 shows a less aggressive management policy that proportionally increases the multiplier based on how late the task is. When the task is only slightly behind schedule (e.g., SPI = 0.90), the project manager does not do anything (i.e., multiplier = 1.0). When the task is moderately behind schedule (e.g., SPI = 0.70), the project manager may add 25% more resources (i.e., multiplier = 1.25). And, when the project is severely behind schedule (e.g., SPI < 0.40), the project manager doubles the assigned resources (i.e., multiplier = 2.0).

In both of the corrective actions that were covered (i.e., adding overtime hours when a task is late and adding resources when a task is late), the goal is to increase the completion rate by increasing either the actual labor hours or the number of resources (or both). A higher completion rate will

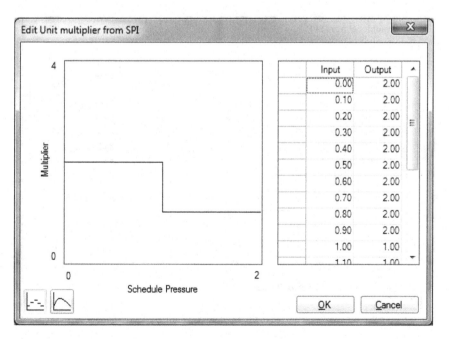

FIGURE 6.10
Aggressive resource policy for SPI.

shorten the task duration and get the task (and project) back on schedule. Note that if a project manager wanted instead to slow down the completion rate on a task because it was actually ahead of schedule, the table functions also accommodate this. In this case, the pmBLOX user would enter multiplier values for SPI values that are greater than 1.0.

Now, let us consider some corrective actions that are associated with CPI (i.e., being over budget or under budget). Typically, project managers only implement corrective actions when the project or task is over budget. In this case, similar to the management policies for SPI, the users can create table functions that define how changes in CPI lead to changes in the amount of overtime hours that are added to a project and the number of resources that are assigned to the task (via a multiplier on the current resources). When costs are high, and a task is over budget, the desire of the project manager is typically to reduce the hours that people are working or reduce the number of people working on the task. Hence, while SPI-related policies typically aim to increase the completion rate (by increasing the effective labor hours through increases in the number of resources or the actual labor hours), CPI-related policies typically aim to reduce the completion rate (i.e., remove resources from the task).

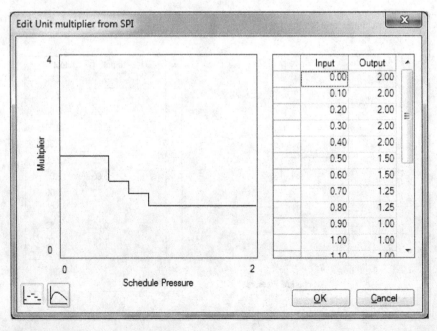

FIGURE 6.11
Proportional resource policy for SPI.

Figures 6.12 through 6.15 show the same four management policies for CPI that are shown in Figures 6.8 through 6.11 for SPI. For instance, Figure 6.12 shows an aggressive policy of changing overtime hours based on CPI, just like Figure 6.8 shows an aggressive policy of changing over-time hours based on SPI. Note, however, that there are some slight differences. For the management policies for CPI for overtime hours (Figures 6.12 and 6.13), the table function shows how many overtime hours to *remove* (not to add). A built-in assumption in the current pmBLOX DPM model is that a project manager would never ask a person to work less than the *normal* day that is set in the calendar (see Chapter 7 for details on setting calendars). Thus, the management policies for CPI only take away any overtime hours that have been added above and beyond the normal workday. For the CPI-based management policies affecting the number of resources (Figures 6.14 and 6.15), the table functions use multipliers on the number of resources, which is the same approach as the SPI-based policies for the number of resources. But, in the CPI-based policies, the multipliers tend to be less than 1 (to indicate a reduction in resources on the task).

One thing readers may notice immediately is that the SPI and CPI tend to work against each other. When the task progress relative to the schedule is

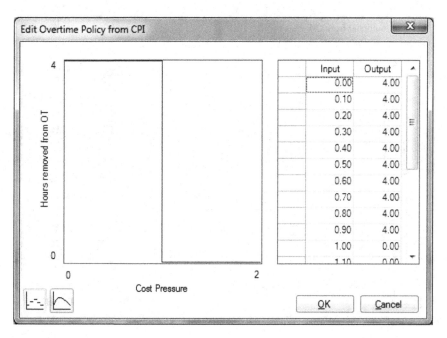

FIGURE 6.12
Aggressive overtime policy for CPI.

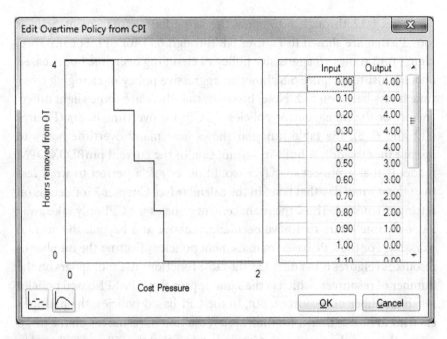

FIGURE 6.13
Proportional overtime policy for CPI.

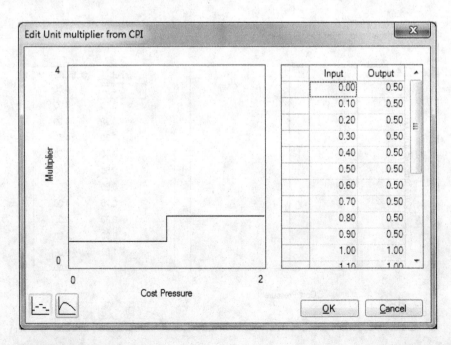

FIGURE 6.14
Aggressive resource policy for CPI.

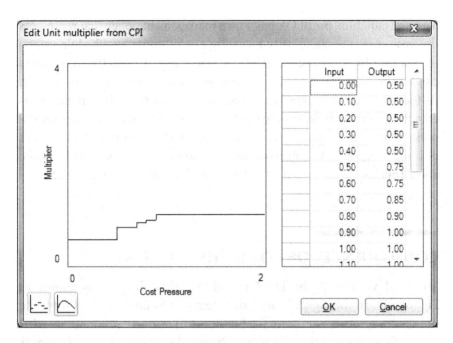

FIGURE 6.15
Proportional resource policy for CPI.

poor (i.e., SPI < 1), the SPI-based policies attempt to shorten the duration by *increasing* the resources that are used on the job (which increases the completion rate). On the other hand, when the task progress relative to cost is poor (i.e., CPI < 1), the CPI-based policies attempt to reduce costs by *removing* the resources that are used on the job (which decreases the completion rate). Hence, if a pmBLOX user implements both SPI-based management policies to control schedule and CPI-based management policies to control cost, in some cases, the changes caused by each of these sets of policies will *cancel* each other out so that the net result is no change at all. For example, if the user has an SPI management policy that adds 2 h of overtime when the task is behind schedule and a CPI management policy that removes 2 h of overtime when the task is over budget, then the addition of 2 h of overtime is canceled out by the removal of 2 h of overtime, and the net result is 0 h of overtime. In a similar example, if the user has an SPI management policy that doubles the number of resources (i.e., multiplier = 2) when the task is behind schedule and a CPI management policy that halves the number of resources (i.e., multiplier = 0.5) when the task is over budget, then the doubling of resources is canceled out by the halving of resources, and the net result is no change in the number of resources. To accommodate this contradiction, pmBLOX has a fifth management policy that represents the project manager's priority for being guided more by schedule priorities (SPI) or by cost priorities (CPI). At one end of the spectrum, the users can set the policy that a task is completely driven by schedule only (SPI). At the other end of the spectrum, the users can set the policy that a task is completely driven by cost only (CPI). In the middle, the users can set the policy that both schedule and cost are considered equally (which may result in competing SPI- and CPI-based policies canceling each other out). (More about this last management policy is covered in Chapter 7, Figure 7.26.)

CONSEQUENCES OF CORRECTIVE ACTIONS

The final version of the DPM model overview diagram is shown in Figure 6.16. In this figure, notice that there are feedback arrows from the number of resources and actual labor hours to resource productivity. This connection indicates that changes in the number of resources and changes in the actual labor hours can cause changes in resource productivity. Typically, the changes that occur are reductions in resource productivity due to assigning too many resources to the task (often called *overmanning* or *overtasking*) or reductions in resource productivity due to fatigue and

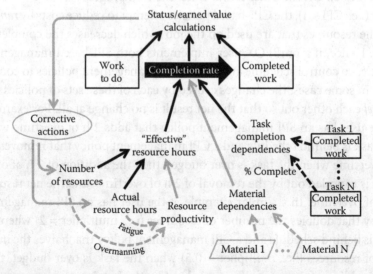

FIGURE 6.16
Basic task model with negative consequences of management actions.

burnout that are caused by assigning people too much overtime. These are common real-world phenomena.

Let us consider a specific example. Suppose that a task is behind schedule. One of the corrective actions described in the "Management Corrective Actions" section in this chapter is to add overtime hours if the task is behind schedule (i.e., SPI < 1). However, in the real world, people are not robots, and eventually, all the overtime will take its toll. As an extreme example, consider someone working 24 h a day for several weeks. Of course, in this example, it is physically impossible to do this. Someone cannot stay awake that long. Without a doubt, we would see a reduction in productivity for this person at some point. In fact, the person's productivity would drop to zero when he or she falls asleep. Even if we stopped assigning overtime to this person, when he or she returns the next day to work a *normal* day, his or her productivity would still be impacted. The fatigue that he or she experiences would take awhile to dissipate and go away. It may take him or her several days to catch up on sleep and be back to full productivity at work. At the other end of examples, consider someone working just 30 min of overtime for a few days. This is not much different from working a normal workday (e.g., 8 h), so the person does not experience much more fatigue than he or she normally experiences. In this case, he or she could probably work several weeks with absolutely no impact or very little impact to productivity. And, when the overtime is removed, and the person comes back to work the following day for a regular workday, he or she has probably fully recovered so that he or she is back to his or her normal level of productivity (since he or she was not excessively burned out or fatigued).

The two phenomena to capture here are the following:

1. The amount of fatigue that a person experiences is proportional to the amount of overtime hours that he or she works (i.e., more overtime hours cause more fatigue), and
2. The recovery period to get back to normal productivity is proportional to the level of fatigue that a person has (i.e., it takes longer to recover from high amounts of fatigue).

The underlying simulation model that captures fatigue is not accessible by the users in pmBLOX. In this model, fatigue accumulates for each overtime hour that a resource works. The dissipation of the level of fatigue (i.e., the recovery from fatigue) is based on the level of fatigue. If the level of fatigue is low (from few overtime hours), recovery is very fast. For example, a person could work several hours of overtime on a single day and come back the next day with minimal (or even zero) fatigue. If he or she worked several hours of overtime for several weeks, the recovery would be much slower when he or she returned to work for the next regular workday, he or she still would be experiencing some high level of fatigue, and it would take several days for the fatigue to completely disappear.

Instead, what is accessible by the users is the definition of how fatigue impacts resource productivity. pmBLOX allows them to capture the productivity impacts in a table function. Figure 6.17 shows the default table function. On the x-axis is the fatigue index, which represents the level of fatigue that is experienced by a resource. If the fatigue index is 0, the resource is completely *fresh* and has no fatigue. If the fatigue index is 100, the resource is completely fatigued (i.e., cannot do anything). On the y-axis is a multiplier on the productivity level for the resource. Two points on this table function will always hold true. When the fatigue index is 0, the multiplier is 1 to indicate no loss of productivity at all; the resource maintains its normal resource productivity. When the fatigue index is 100, the multiplier is 0 to indicate that no work can be done at all. These are the upper-left and lower-right corners of the table function. In between those

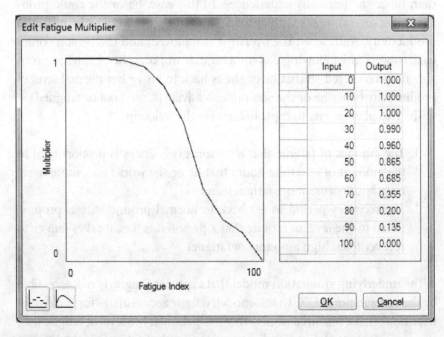

FIGURE 6.17
Example fatigue multiplier table.

two endpoints, the user has the flexibility to assign whatever impact on productivity seems appropriate. By default, pmBLOX suggests the relationship in Figure 6.17. Notice that there is no decrease in the multiplier until the fatigue index reaches 30, and at that point, there is only a 1% loss in productivity (i.e., the multiplier is 0.99). Thus, even when the resource is 30% fatigued, that resource is still at 99% of whatever its normal productivity level is. This is very conservative and suggests that the resource can work a fair amount of overtime for an extended period of time with almost no impact on productivity. The user has the option of making this relationship more severe such that productivity losses occur immediately when there is very little fatigue. Or, the user can go to the other extreme and set the multiplier equal to 1 for all the values of the fatigue index to indicate that the resource does not suffer from fatigue at all.

Similar to the productivity losses due to fatigue, Figure 6.16 shows that resource productivity is impacted by the number of resources. Simply put, for some tasks and for some types of work, there can be *too many cooks in the kitchen*, and there is a lot of *stepping on toes*. Coordination is difficult, and work progress grinds to a halt. Or, for some tasks, it may be impossible to add more resources due to physical constraints (e.g., only two plumbers can fit in the space under a sink). By default, pmBLOX sets this table function so that there is no impact due to overmanning (i.e., multiplier = 1 for all values). Figure 6.18 shows a more realistic relationship between overmanning and the impact on productivity. In Figure 6.18, the overmanning ratio is on the x-axis, and the productivity multiplier is on the y-axis (similar to Figure 6.17). The overmanning ratio is the current number of resources that are assigned to the task divided by the desired number of resources for the task (which is set when assigning resources to tasks). For example, if the desired number of resources (for this particular resource type) is 2, and a management policy caused this number of resources to increase to 4 (e.g., doubling resources because the task was behind schedule), then the overmanning ratio is 2. Or, if the desired number of resources is 2, and a management policy caused this number of resources to increase to 3, then the overmanning ratio is 1.5.

Figure 6.18 shows that if the current number of resources is triple the desired number of resources (i.e., overmanning ratio = 3), the multiplier on resource productivity drops to 0.50 (i.e., half as productive). In this particular example table function, 0.50 is the lowest that the multiplier drops to. So, no matter how many additional resources are added to this task, the productivity of these resources will never drop below 50% of each

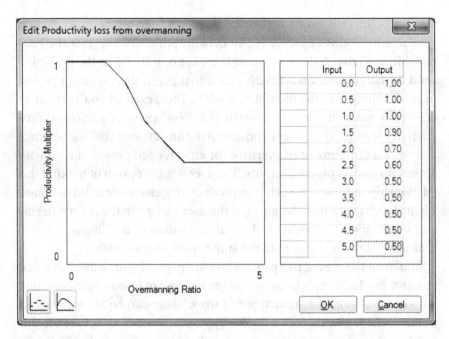

Edit Productivity loss from overmanning

Input	Output
0.0	1.00
0.5	1.00
1.0	1.00
1.5	0.90
2.0	0.70
2.5	0.60
3.0	0.50
3.5	0.50
4.0	0.50
4.5	0.50
5.0	0.50

FIGURE 6.18
Example productivity loss multiplier table.

resource's normal productivity level. Note that the user could set the productivity multiplier to 0, if desired, to show that there is a limit to the number of resources that can be added to this task. In the table function in Figure 6.18, the first productivity impact comes when the overmanning ratio is 1.5 (which means 50% additional resources above the desired *number of resources*). At this point, the multiplier on *resource productivity* drops to 0.90 (i.e., 90% of normal productivity level).

INTEGRATED VIEW OF pmBLOX MODEL

The previous sections of this chapter introduced many of the details of the underlying DPM simulation model found in pmBLOX, and Figure 6.16 provides the full view of the underlying model for a single task in pmBLOX. Figure 6.19 provides an example integrated view of how multiple tasks would be simulated together in pmBLOX. In this very simple example, there are five tasks labeled A through E, each represented by a small version of the task-level graphic seen in Figure 6.16. The thick

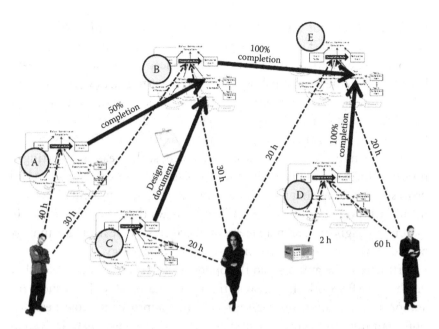

FIGURE 6.19
The integrated view of pmBLOX.

solid arrows represent the dependencies among tasks, which may be a percent completion dependency on a predecessor task or a material dependency from another task that creates a material. Task A requires only one resource for 40 h of work. Task B requires the same resource as Task A but for only 30 h, along with another resource for 30 h. However, Task B cannot start until Task A is 50% complete, and Task C creates its design document (which is needed as an input material into Task B). The resource for Task C is also required for Task B and Task E. Task D requires a human resource (for 60 hours) and a piece of test equipment for 2 h. And so on.

With a graphic like the one in Figure 6.19, it is easy to see how complicated project planning is in the real world, along with how complicated it is to realistically estimate cost and schedule (i.e., duration). Imagine if this project were 50 tasks or 100 tasks, which in today's business world is not considered a large project. Consequently, it is easy to see that the methods developed back in the 1950s (i.e., PERT/CPM) are woefully insufficient for capturing the complexities necessary for realistic planning and management of large, complex projects.

For decades, today's PM tools have been built around this CPM *engine* that is less than ideal and, in many cases, outright incorrect. It is difficult, if not impossible, for the manufacturers of the current PM tools to scrap this engine and start over. As a result, more and more fixes are added on top of a broken foundation. For example, concepts like *lead* and *lag* have been added to the basic finish-to-start (FS), start-to-start (SS), etc. dependencies among tasks to account for the fact that sometimes a successor task does not fit exactly into one of these major dependencies. But, these fixes are just shell games that make the major flaws of PERT/CPM worse. Or, user-friendliness features have been added, such as easier exporting of project information into other office tools (such as spreadsheets or word processors) or accessing files via the Internet. Yet, these usability improvements still do not address the underlying flaws that lead to mistakes in planning, diagnosis, and management of projects. 60-year-old technology provided over the Internet is still 60-year-old technology.

Fortunately, the authors had the opportunity to start with a clean slate on the DARPA work that created the DPM and pmBLOX. As such, the authors feel that this is the beginning of a new approach to project estimation, planning, and management that harnesses the power of today's computers and the new knowledge that the project management community has gained over the last couple of decades.

A FINAL NOTE ON THE DPM MODEL

It should be noted that the simulation model covered in this chapter and embedded in the pmBLOX PM software is not the *definitive* DPM model. As discussed in Chapters 1 through 5, the DPM embodies a set of philosophies about how to make project planning and estimation more realistic by focusing on resources, management corrective actions, and the impacts of corrective actions on resources (via productivity levels). The main purpose of the DPM is to offer a better alternative to the outdated and insufficient duration-based methods that are the foundation of most current PM tools on the market. Indeed, this is the first official publication of any formal DPM-oriented model, and pmBLOX is the first commercially available tool that employs extensive DPM features. But, this model of the DPM is not the end-all model. On the contrary, it is only the beginning model. Readers are encouraged to refine and expand on the model that is presented in this book by joining the forums and discussions at http://www.dynamicprogressmethod.com.

7

Overview of pmBLOX

INTRODUCTION

Chapters 1 through 6 addressed the theory and algorithms defining the Dynamic Progress Method (DPM). We now turn our attention to putting the DPM to work using project management software called pmBLOX®. A trial version of pmBLOX is available as a free download on http://www .pmblox.com. Additional tutorials and videos are also available at the website.

By the end of this chapter, the reader will be able to

- Navigate the main views within pmBLOX
- Create a new project plan in pmBLOX
- Populate a task with resources defining a project plan
- Configure tasks and resources applying DPM principles
- Understand the differences between CPM- and DPM-based planning methods

INSTALLING AND RUNNING pmBLOX

Once you have downloaded pmBLOX, double-click on the installer to copy the program to your computer. (*Note*: pmBLOX requires a Microsoft Windows operating system to run.) After the installation process completes, you can run pmBLOX by selecting the program from your Start menu or desktop shortcut or by double-clicking on the application file (located in your C:\Program Files\pmBLOX directory). Once the program loads, you will see an empty project view (see Figure 7.1).

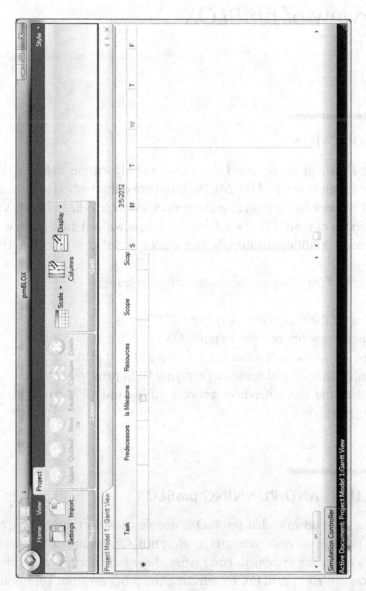

FIGURE 7.1

A blank pmBLOX project plan showing the Gantt view.

pmBLOX should look familiar to anybody who has used other project management software. This is by design—while the underlying *engine* that performs the calculations to determine task durations, resource utilizations, etc., is fundamentally different, the inputs used to define the plan are not. (There are some exceptions, as you shall soon see, as the DPM method includes inputs that other project planning tools fail to acknowledge.)

pmBLOX groups common functions with the ribbon bars at the top of the application window. The first two, "Home" and "View," provide common controls that are used by different views into your plan's data. Depending on which view you are using, there may be other tabs containing control options that are specific to the view.

The default view for any new project plan is the Gantt view. In this view, you define the tasks that comprise your project. The other views are the following:

- *Resources*—where you define the labor, equipment, and materials that are needed for your project
- *Calendars*—where you define the work hours a resource is available
- *Management policies*—where you define different rule sets for how tasks respond to cost and schedule pressure
- *Reports*—where you view the project's simulation results (e.g., resource utilization, costs)

EXAMPLE 1—CREATING YOUR FIRST PROJECT PLAN

Before getting into all of the details of pmBLOX's implementation of the DPM, we will create the most basic project plan so that you can see how to run a simulation to evaluate your project. If you have a blank project, like the one shown in Figure 7.1, you can use that; otherwise, you will want to create a new project file. Click on the application icon in the top left, and then choose "New," or click on the blank document icon to the right of the application menu (Figure 7.2).

If you choose the "New" menu command, a dialog will appear (Figure 7.3), letting you select what type of new document to create. pmBLOX uses a generalized simulation platform called SimBLOX™ so that some users of pmBLOX will have additional document options. Now that you have

FIGURE 7.2
Creating a new pmBLOX file.

a new document, click in the first row of the Gantt view, and type in a name for the project task, for example, "Task 1." Next, tab over to the Scope column, and enter the task duration—for our example, we will enter 40h, indicating that the task will take 40 h of productive work to complete (Figure 7.4).

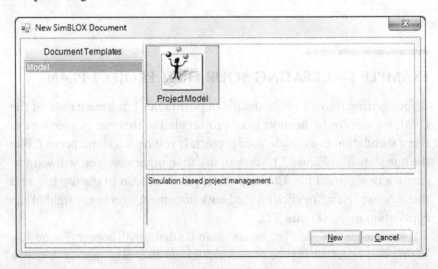

FIGURE 7.3
Selecting a new pmBLOX model.

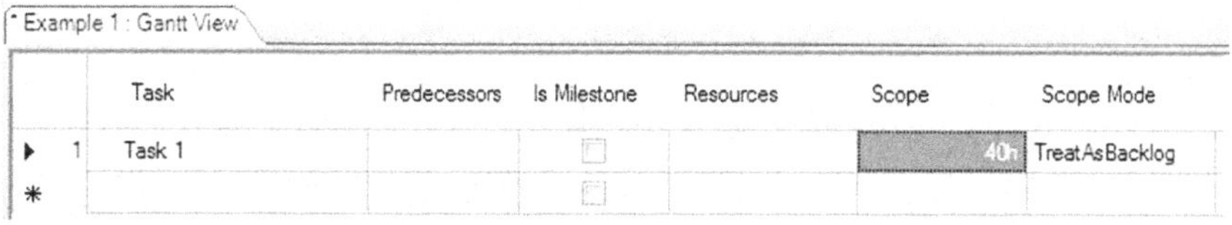

		Task	Predecessors	Is Milestone	Resources	Scope	Scope Mode
▶	1	Task 1		☐		40h	TreatAsBacklog
✳				☐			

FIGURE 7.4
Defining a single task.

Unlike other project management tools you may have used, in pmBLOX, the Gantt chart does not automatically update. You will need to run the DPM simulation to get an updated Gantt chart. At the bottom of the pmBLOX application is a docked window titled "Simulation Controller." This is where you run the simulation. Notice that the document title shows the name of your newly created document (e.g., Project Model 1). If you have multiple project plans open, you can control which you wish to simulate by selecting it from the list of open projects and clicking the "Run" button. If you had not saved your file previously, you will be prompted to save your new project plan prior to running the simulation. For our example, we will name the file "Example 1." After saving the file, the simulation runs, displaying the results that are shown in Figure 7.5.

In the Simulation Controller window, informational messages are displayed.

The project's default start date is set to the current date. To change the project start day, click on the "Settings" button on the Project tab in the Ribbon bar (Figure 7.6). You can ignore the other settings on the dialog for the time being. We will revisit these options in Chapter 8.

EXAMPLE 2—DEFINING A TASK RESOURCE

In our first example, the task work scope was set with no resources that are assigned. In order to take full advantage of the DPM methodology, tasks that are not simple duration events (e.g., time for paint to dry) should always assign resources. The easiest way to define a resource for a task is to simply type in the resource name in the resource column, followed by the expected work effort that is required by the resource. In this example, we will enter in the resource name "Moe" and indicate that it will take Moe 40 h (40 h) to complete this task. When you enter in the resource name, the original scope resets to 0 h, ensuring that you do not inadvertently assign a work scope

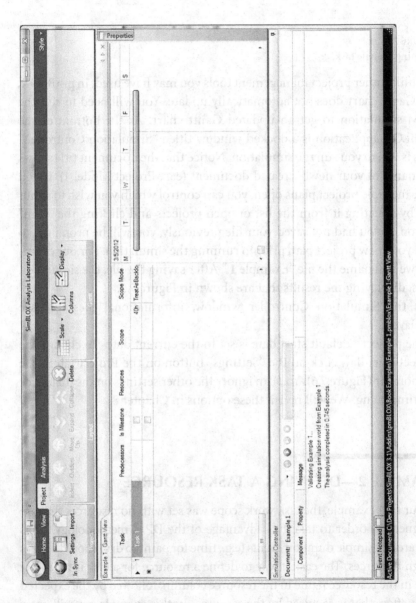

FIGURE 7.5
Simulating a single task.

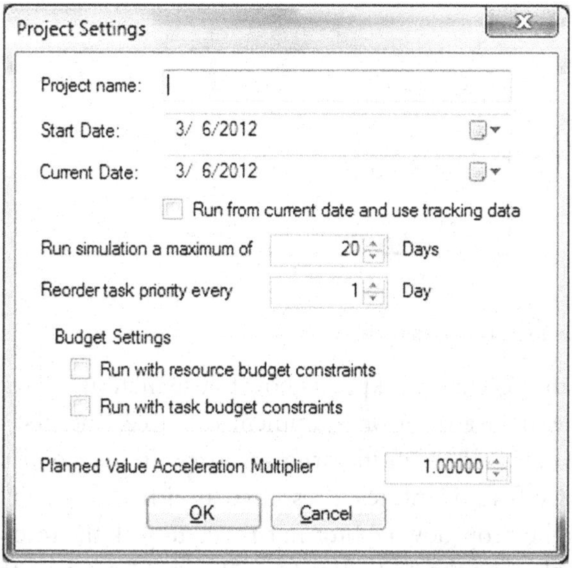

FIGURE 7.6
Project Settings dialog.

that is not related to the resource. When entering in the work scope, you can define it in terms of hours (h), days (d), or weeks (w).

Your Gantt view should look like the one in Figure 7.7.

Note that in the Project ribbon, the "In Sync" button appears disabled when the plan data have changed. Double-check the In Sync status to determine whether or not a new simulation needs to be run; otherwise, your simulation results may not reflect the current plan inputs. Before running the simulation, let us look at the resource view. Click on the "View" tab in the ribbon bar, and then select "Resources" (Figure 7.8).

The resource view shows the labor, equipment, and material resources that are defined in your project. Typing "Moe" into the Gantt view automatically creates a named resource and establishes the default properties for that resource (Figure 7.9).

The resource view has two input areas. The top grid defines both labor and equipment resources. The bottom grid defines project materials.

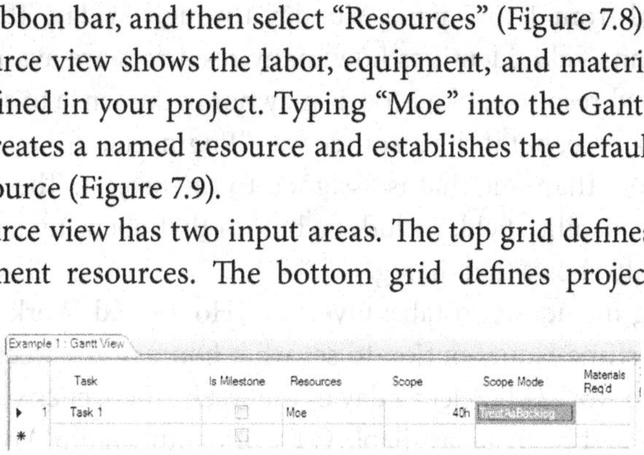

FIGURE 7.7
Adding a named resource to your task.

FIGURE 7.8
Changing views to display resources.

(Example 8 in this chapter explains how to use materials.) There are eight properties defining a labor or equipment resource. The first column, the Resource Name field, identifies the resource. The second column, the Resource Type field, identifies a resource as either Labor or Equipment. You can use the drop-down editor in the cell to pick the resource type, or you can simply type the first letter (e.g., "L" or "E" when in the cell to set the type). The third column, the Hourly Rate field, defines the hourly cost for the resource. The DPM uses the cost information to perform its earned value calculations and establish any potential cost or schedule pressures as a function of cost. The fourth column, the Overtime (OT) rate multiplier (OT Rate Mult.) field, establishes the cost per OT hour as a function of the regular hourly work rate. By default, this value is 1.5, indicating a time-and-a-half model for OT. In this example then, Moe's OT rate would be $15.00 per hour. The fifth column, the Calendar field, sets the calendar that is used to establish resource availability. The default "Standard" calendar establishes a 40-h workweek, with work hours from 9 a.m. to 12 noon and from 1 to 5 p.m., Monday through Friday. The sixth column, the Units field, identifies how many resources are available. When using a named resource, like Moe, it may not make sense to specify more than one resource, but if the resource was "Engineers," for example, there might be more than one that is assigned to the project. The seventh column, the Availability field, includes a button that opens up a custom editor. Figure 7.10 shows that dialog.

The dialog includes two tabs: Overtime Hours and Work Exceptions. Use the Overtime Hours option to set what hours of the week a resource is available to work OT. Select a day of the week. Then, click on an hour to toggle between it being an available OT work hour (in pink) or a nonwork hour. The gray hours show the scheduled, non-OT hours the resource is scheduled for work, based on the resource calendar that is selected.

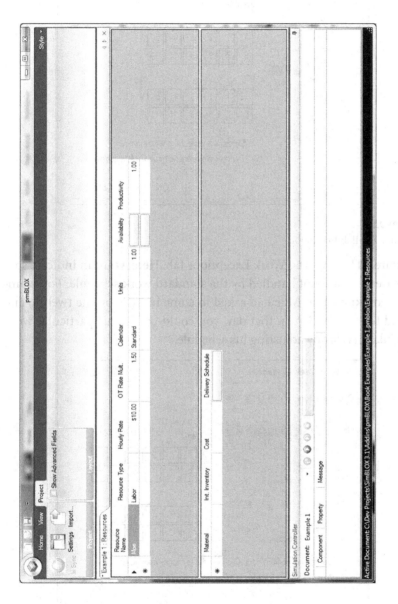

FIGURE 7.9
The resource view.

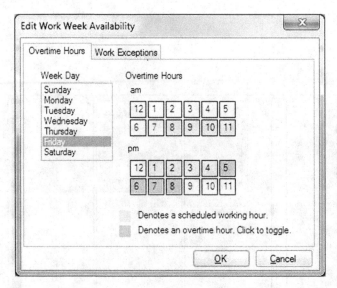

FIGURE 7.10
Resource Availability dialog.

Figure 7.11 shows the Work Exceptions tab. Here, you can indicate special cases that are not handled by the standard work schedule. For example, if you knew that Moe had asked to come in early on the twelfth, and he had to leave by 2 p.m. that day, you could update his particular work schedule that day by adjusting his schedule.

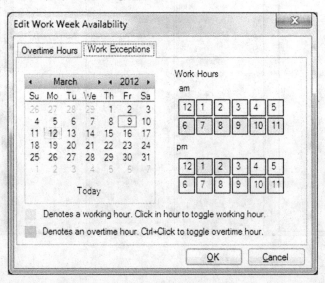

FIGURE 7.11
Adjusting a resource's work schedule.

The eighth and final input column is the Productivity field. There are upcoming examples, so we will defer the discussion for the time being.

With Moe's settings configured, switch back to the Gantt view, and rerun the simulation. At first glance, the results look identical to our first example—the task takes five days to complete. However, if we go to the reports view (View tab, select Reports; Figure 7.12), we can view the details about the work that Moe accomplished that were not available in Example 1. Before examining the simulation results, let us look at how you use the Reports view. The Reports view allows you to explore the details behind the project plan. While the Gantt chart provides the big picture of your project, you will want to use the Reports view to understand what is happening inside each task. Once the Reports view is showing, use the Project ribbon bar to select the report type, style, and time scale. Figure 7.12 shows the options that are available for each of the controls. Time scales for results are daily, weekly, monthly, quarterly, or annually. In general, the more complex the project, the longer the time horizon that you will want

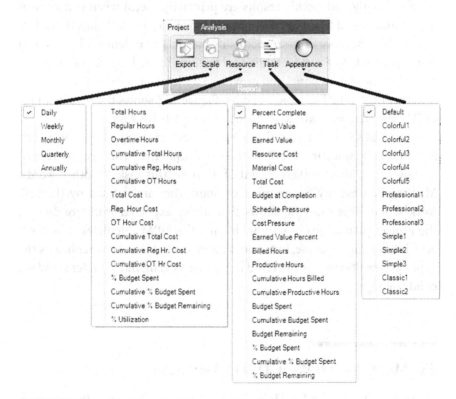

FIGURE 7.12
Report settings.

	A	B	C	D	E	F	G	H
	Project Model 1 : Gantt View	Example 2 : Reports						
1	Days	3/4/2012	3/5/2012	3/6/2012	3/7/2012	3/8/2012	3/9/2012	3/10/2012
2	Moe [Labor]	0	8	8	8	8	8	0
3	Total	0	8	8	8	8	8	0

FIGURE 7.13
Moe's hours worked each day.

	A	B	C	D	E	F	G	H
	Project Model 1 : Gantt View	" Example 2 : Reports						
1	Days	3/4/2012	3/5/2012	3/6/2012	3/7/2012	3/8/2012	3/9/2012	3/10/2012
2	Moe [Labor]	0	8	16	24	32	40	40
3	Total	0	8	16	24	32	40	40

FIGURE 7.14
Cumulative total hours worked.

to select. Daily and weekly results are primarily useful when you are trying to understand how the DPM results lead to specific task durations. You can modify the report appearance using one of the predefined themes. You can export data to Excel for additional analysis by clicking on the "Export" button in the ribbon panel and providing a file name for the data file.

Returning to the Example 2 results, Figure 7.13 shows the regular (non-OT) hours that were worked by Moe to complete his task.

Figure 7.14 shows the cumulative hours that were worked by Moe, which is viewable by selecting the Resources → Cumulative Total Hours report. It shows that Moe worked a total of 40 h on this task. In other words, Moe worked exactly the number of hours that are defined by the task work scope. This example shows that under expected work conditions, the project plan aligns exactly with what the DPM calculates. It is not a very interesting example, but it does confirm that the DPM replicates the expected results that are provided by CPM-based methods under standard conditions.

EXAMPLE 3—PRODUCTIVITY IMPACTS

Example 3 shows how the DPM differs from the CPM when dealing with less-than-expected productivity. Assume that Moe is a new employee and is still learning his way around the organization. We expect that the first task we assign to Moe will take him longer than our other employees as he learns company practices and procedures. We can account for this by adjusting Moe's productivity. Relative to the experienced employees, Moe will provide 50 min of productive work for every hour that is spent on the task. In other words, Moe is 50/60 min or 83% productive.

Open up the Resource view, set Moe's productivity to 0.83, and rerun your simulation. In Example 2, it took Moe five workdays to complete Task 1. Now, however, because Moe is not working as efficiently as we would ideally like, the task takes an extra 9 h to complete. (Technically, it took 48.2 h, but the pmBLOX simulation has a resolution of a single hour, so the extra 20 min is treated as a full work hour.) The task started Monday morning, and instead of being completed at 5:00 p.m. on Friday, Moe now completes his task the following Tuesday at 9 a.m. Returning to the reports view, we will look at four different reports to understand Moe's progress:

1. Resource report "Total Hours" (Figure 7.15a)
2. Task report "Productive Hours" (Figure 7.15b)
3. Task report "Percent Complete" (Figure 7.15c)
4. Task report "Total Cost" (Figure 7.15d)

The resource report shows that Moe has billed 49 h, roughly 22% greater than the defined work scope of 40 h. The reduced rate of backlog

DPM VERSUS CPM/PERT

PERT techniques are frequently used in conjunction with the CPM to account for task duration uncertainty. The problem with the PERT technique is that it masks the underlying behavioral dynamics that result in different task durations. There is no correlation between the rate of task completion and the real-world behaviors resulting in altered project schedules.

The DPM, in contrast, allows you to explicitly evaluate the potential impact of resource behavior on the overall project plan. Productivity is just one of the key influencers on overall project outcome when using the DPM method—dynamically changing productivity rates in response to real environmental conditions results in a more realistic evaluation of project plans.

	A	B	C	D	E	F	G	H	I	J	K	L
1	Days	3/4/2012	3/5/2012	3/6/2012	3/7/2012	3/8/2012	3/9/2012	3/10/2012	3/11/2012	3/12/2012	3/13/2012	3/14/2012
2	Moe [Labor]	0	8	8	8	8	8	8	0	0	1	0
3	Total	0	8	8	8	8	8	8	0	0	1	0

(a)

	A	B	C	D	E	F	G	H	I	J	K	L
1	Days	3/4/2012	3/5/2012	3/6/2012	3/7/2012	3/8/2012	3/9/2012	3/10/2012	3/11/2012	3/12/2012	3/13/2012	3/14/2012
2	Task 1	0	7	7	7	7	7	7	0	0	1	0

(b)

	A	B	C	D	E	F	G	H	I	J	K	L
1	Days	3/4/2012	3/5/2012	3/6/2012	3/7/2012	3/8/2012	3/9/2012	3/10/2012	3/11/2012	3/12/2012	3/13/2012	3/14/2012
2	Task 1	0 %	17 %	33 %	50 %	66 %	83 %	83 %	83 %	100 %	100 %	0 %
3	Total											

(c)

	A	B	C	D	E	F	G	H	I	J	K	L
1	Days	3/4/2012	3/5/2012	3/6/2012	3/7/2012	3/8/2012	3/9/2012	3/10/2012	3/11/2012	3/12/2012	3/13/2012	3/14/2012
2	Task 1	$0	$80	$160	$240	$320	$400	$400	$400	$400	$480	$490	$0
3	Total												$0

(d)

FIGURE 7.15
Resource report "Total Hours" (a), Task report "Productive Hours" (b), "Percent Complete" (c), "Total Cost" (d).

completion is shown in Figure 7.15b. Similarly, Figure 7.15c presents the percent completion of the task on a daily basis. Notice that Moe does not complete any work over the weekend. The last table shows the total cost for Moe's time. His hourly rate of $10 translates into the $490 cost.

EXAMPLE 4—VARYING PRODUCTIVITY IMPACTS

Example 3 highlights the impact of productivity on overall work performance, but it is admittedly overly simplistic. It is unreasonable to expect Moe to operate at less-than-full productive capacity during his entire time on the project, especially in cases where there may be dozens of tasks requiring Moe's services. Let us look at a more realistic example. In this example, we will address varying productivity over the course of the workweek and in response to task complexity. Open the Resource view, and select the Project tab. Check the box that reads, "Show Advanced Fields" (Figure 7.16).

Three new input columns appear in the view: (1) Unit Schedule, (2) Productivity Schedule, and (3) Fatigue. For this example, we are only concerned with Productivity Schedule. Click on the button in the Productivity Schedule column for Moe. A dialog box like the one shown in Figure 7.17 appears.

This dialog lets you set varying productivity rates over the course of a project. The productivity rates can be set for three levels of task complexity: low, medium, and high, and they can be set for any day of the week. To set productivities, click on the desired date, and then enter in the desired productivity values. You can hover over any day in the calendar to see the set values without having to click and select the date. When you set a productivity value, it remains in effect until a new value overrides it. For example, the defaults for Moe are initialized to productivity rates of 1.0 for every day. In this example, we are going to make two changes. First, we are going to distinguish between a complex task and a medium- or low-complexity task. We will assume that Moe is less productive when working on complex tasks, so we will set the productivity for highly complex tasks to 0.875. In other words, we can expect to get about 7 h of productive work for a day's effort when Moe is dealing with something more complicated.

Next, we want to account for the fact that Moe ends up spending roughly 2 h each Monday answering e-mails, catching up with colleagues,

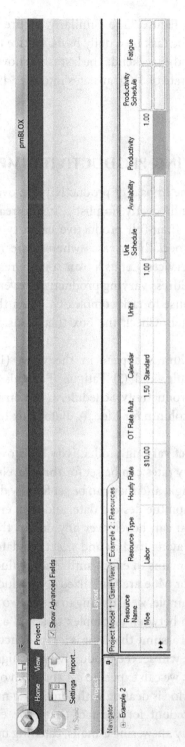

FIGURE 7.16

Advanced Resource fields.

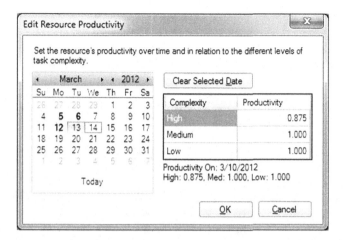

FIGURE 7.17
Resource productivity schedule.

and sitting in on meetings. In order to account for these nonproductive activities, we will set the productivity for March 5 and 12 to the following values: High: 0.625, Medium: 0.75, and Low: 0.75. The productivity values are returned to the expected values of 0.875, 1.0, and 1.0 on March 6 and 13. Recapping how the productivity rates are calculated, on Mondays, we know that 2 of every 8 h Moe works are *lost* to miscellaneous activities in the office. Therefore, the medium- and low-complexity task productivity is 6 productive hours/8 work hours or 0.75. Accounting for the extra lost hour for complex tasks, Moe completes 5 productive hours for each 8 work hours or 0.625. Rerun the simulation, and view the results. We see that the five-day task now adds an additional 3 h to the overall project duration, finishing up at 11 a.m. on the following Monday. Figure 7.18a and b shows the billed and productive hours for Moe.

Return to the Gantt view, and scroll over to the Complexity column. Change the Task 1 complexity from "Medium" to "High," and rerun the simulation. Use the Reports view to examine the Resource Total Hours and Task Productive Hours reports (Figure 7.19a and b). Notice that Moe's productive hours are five on the two Mondays when the task is active. Notice, too, that the task now ends a day later.

Lastly, for this example, let us change the start date of the project from a Monday to a Tuesday. Shifting the task start by one day reduces the total billed hours from 51 to 48 because only one of Moe's least productive days factored in to the task work.

	A	B	C	D	E	F	G	H	I	J	K
1	Days	3/4/2012	3/5/2012	3/6/2012	3/7/2012	3/8/2012	3/9/2012	3/10/2012	3/11/2012	3/12/2012	3/13/2012
2	Task 1	0	8	8	8	8	8	0	0	3	0

(a)

	A	B	C	D	E	F	G	H	I	J	K
1	Days	3/4/2012	3/5/2012	3/6/2012	3/7/2012	3/8/2012	3/9/2012	3/10/2012	3/11/2012	3/12/2012	3/13/2012
2	Task 1	0	6	8	8	8	8	0	0	2	0

(b)

FIGURE 7.18
Billed hours (a) and Productive hours (b).

	A	B	C	D	E	F	G	H	I	J	K	L
1	Days	3/4/2012	3/5/2012	3/6/2012	3/7/2012	3/8/2012	3/9/2012	3/10/2012	3/11/2012	3/12/2012	3/13/2012	3/14/2012
2	Moe [Labor]	0	8	8	8	8	8	0	0	8	3	0
3	Total	0	8	8	8	8	8	0	0	8	3	0

(a)

	A	B	C	D	E	F	G	H	I	J	K	L
1	Days	3/4/2012	3/5/2012	3/6/2012	3/7/2012	3/8/2012	3/9/2012	3/10/2012	3/11/2012	3/12/2012	3/13/2012	3/14/2012
2	Task 1	0	5	7	7	7	7	0	0	5	3	0
3	Total											

(b)

FIGURE 7.19
Resource Total Hours report (a) and Task Productive Hours report (b).

DPM VERSUS CPM

Project management tools based on the CPM have no way to account for the variations of resource productivity. In fact, they typically ignore concepts like variable worker productivity. In a tool other than pmBLOX, you could try to approximate the behavior that is shown in the previous example by indicating that Moe was only available to work 6 h on Mondays. However, doing that fails to account for the cost of those unproductive hours—Moe is still being paid for his 40 h of work; it is just not reflected in his productive output on the project. In Chapter 8, you will see how productivity losses combined with budgetary constraints can lead to altered project outcome.

EXAMPLE 5—RESPONDING TO REDUCED PRODUCTIVITY

A good project manager monitors task progress and adjusts resources accordingly. The DPM uses the earned value calculations in conjunction with defined management policies to get a project back on task. Building on the last example, let us look at how Moe could get back to the target schedule despite his lost hours during his regular workweek. First, return the start date of the project back to Monday. Next, open up the Resource view, and select Moe's input row. Click on the Availability button to open up the Editor dialog. We are going to indicate that Moe is available to work up to 2 h of OT Monday through Friday and up to 4 h of OT on Saturday. To set the resource's OT hours, first, select the day of the week, and then click on the hours that the resource is available to work. Figure 7.20a shows what the OT hours look like for one of the weekdays, while Figure 7.20b presents the OT hours that are set for Saturday.

Select "OK" to save your changes, and rerun the simulation. Looking at either the Gantt view or the reports view, you will notice that Task 1 still required 51 work hours and was completed at the same time even though we said that Moe could work OT. Why? There were no changes in task outcome because the rules governing OT never got invoked. This is where management policies come into play. Management policies define how tasks respond to cost or schedule pressures. In pmBLOX, you can define management rule sets and apply those rules to the project as a whole or

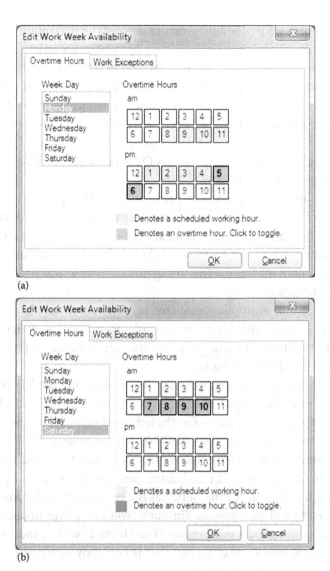

FIGURE 7.20
Setting OT availability for a weekday (a) and Saturday (b).

even override the policies on a per-task basis. There are four management policies comprising each rule set:

1. OT policy for schedule pressure (SPI)
2. OT policy from cost pressure (CPI)
3. Unit multiplier from schedule pressure (SPI)
4. Unit multiplier from cost pressure (CPI)

The OT policy for schedule pressure defines the maximum number of hours per day of OT that a resource should work as a function of schedule pressure. Recall from Chapter 4 (earned value) that schedule pressure is calculated by comparing the actual rate of work progress against the expected rate of work progress. As the actual work rate slows down, you can define a policy to have resources work OT in order to catch up. The OT policy from cost pressure offers a balancing force to the OT policy for schedule pressure. This policy reduces OT hours as the task budget begins to exceed the expected cost.

Unit multiplier from schedule pressure is another policy that looks at the actual versus expected work rates. Use this policy to add additional resources to a task as it falls behind schedule. There is a practical limit to how many resources can be added without affecting overall productivity. You can account for this overmanning productivity loss as part of the task resource definition.

Lastly, the unit multiplier from cost pressure serves as the counterbalance to the unit multiplier from schedule pressure. This policy seeks to reduce the number of extra resources that are assigned to the task as it begins to exceed the task budget.

Open up the management policies view by selecting the Views tab and then selecting the "Mgmt Policies" view option. Figure 7.21 shows an example of the policies editor. On the left-hand side of the view is a list of the predefined policies that are available in your project. The "Is Default" column identifies the policy rule set that is applied to all tasks in a project unless overridden at the task level. You can create a new policy set by typing in the name of the policy at the bottom of the list and editing the entries to suit your needs. Similarly, you can delete unused policies by selecting the policy and pressing the Delete key. It cannot delete the default management policy or one that is currently assigned to a project task.

To the right is a graphical editor that lets you establish the behavior of the management policy rule. Select a rule from the drop-down list at the top of the view, and then edit the values for the selected rule.

You can define management policies using an input–output function. The input is the ratio of the current schedule pressure relative to the expected schedule pressure of the ratio of current cost pressure relative to the expected cost pressure. As the expected value drops below the expected value, the ratio goes below 1.0. When the current value is the same as the expected, the ratio is 1.0. This condition indicates that the task

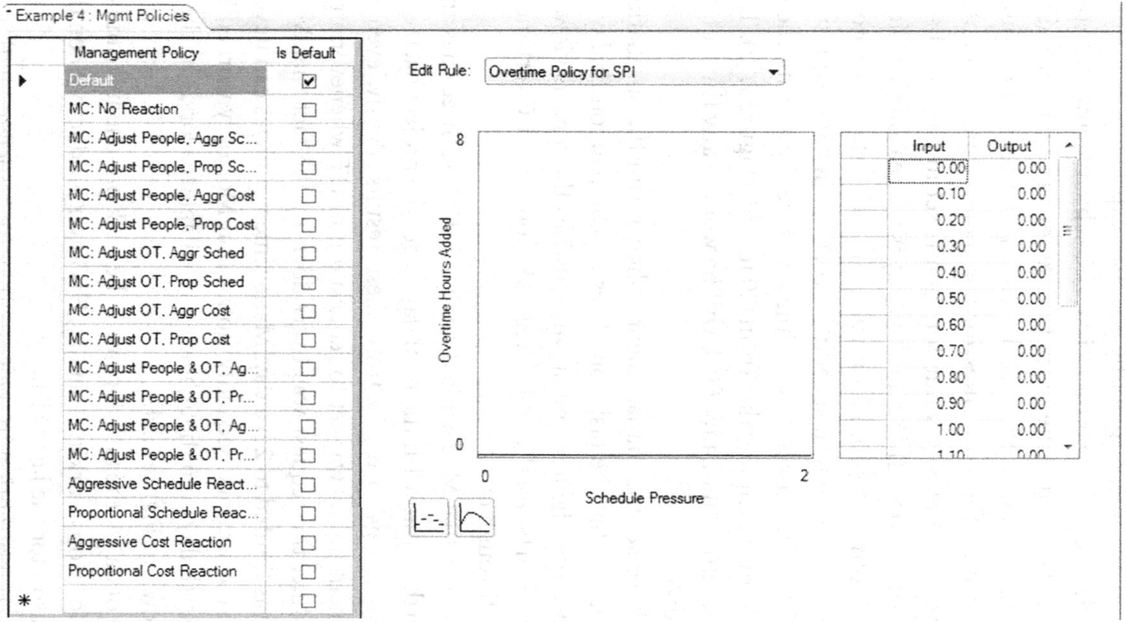

FIGURE 7.21

The management policies view.

is neither behind nor ahead of schedule in the case of the schedule pressure ratio and that the task is neither ahead nor behind budget in the case of the cost pressure ratio. When the schedule pressure ratio is greater than 1.0, the task is ahead of schedule. Similarly, when the cost pressure ratio is greater than 1.0, the task is spending less than expected.

During each hour of the simulation, the schedule and cost pressure ratios are calculated, and the output value for OT hours or additional resources are assigned to the task based on the defined output value. Examining each of the four rules for the default management policy, you will see that the output value for each is set to 0.0 for all schedule and cost pressure ratios. This default policy is the reason that Moe never worked OT in our last simulation run. The rules state that no matter how much the task is behind schedule, no OT hours are requested. Edit the default OT policy for SPI (schedule pressure) by setting the output value to "4" for every input value from 0.0 to 0.90 (Figure 7.22). This rule states that a maximum of 4 h of OT will be worked any time a task falls behind schedule.

Once you have set the management policy, rerun the simulation. The Gantt view shows that the task completes at 6:00 p.m. on Friday. Moe is able to get back on schedule, but at what cost? In the reports view, look at the resource reports Total Hours, Regular Hours, and Overtime Hours (Figure 7.23a through c).

The results show that Moe worked 2 h of OT the first three days and then 1.5 h the fourth day and 1 h the final day to get the project back on track. There are two things to notice from these results. Firstly, even though the management policy was set to request 4 h of OT whenever a task fell behind schedule, the request was overridden by the fact that Moe's OT availability was limited to 2 h a day. Management policies can never override resource constraints. Secondly, notice that Moe only worked 1.5 h of OT on the fourth day even though he was available to work 2 h. The reason for this is shown in Figure 7.24.

By the end of day 4, the task appears to be back on schedule, and once at that point, Moe stops working that day. His lower productivity on the final day is the reason for the last OT hour.

Let us turn our attention to the costs that are associated with completing this single task. The task scope is set to 40 h, and our billed rate for Moe is $10.00. This means that the expected cost to complete Task 1 is $400.00. Moe's cost escalates to $15.00 per hour whenever he works OT. The total cost for the accelerated task climbs to $527.00. You can view this

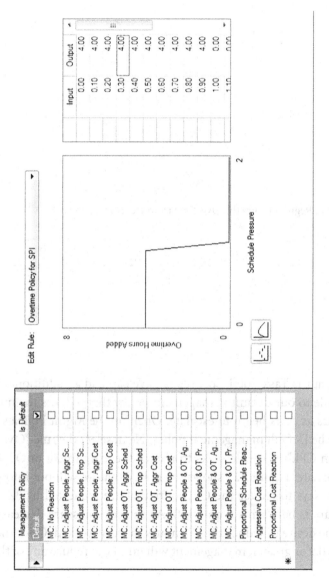

FIGURE 7.22
Setting the default OT policy.

	A	B	C	D	E	F	G	H	I
1	Days	3/4/2012	3/5/2012	3/6/2012	3/7/2012	3/8/2012	3/9/2012	3/10/2012	3/11/2012
2	Moe [Labor]	0.0	10.0	10.0	10.0	9.5	9.0	0.0	0.0
3	Total	0.0	10.0	10.0	10.0	9.5	9.0	0.0	0.0

(a)

	A	B	C	D	E	F	G	H	I
1	Days	3/4/2012	3/5/2012	3/6/2012	3/7/2012	3/8/2012	3/9/2012	3/10/2012	3/11/2012
2	Moe [Labor]	0.0	8.0	8.0	8.0	8.0	8.0	0.0	0.0
3	Total	0.0	8.0	8.0	8.0	8.0	8.0	0.0	0.0

(b)

	A	B	C	D	E	F	G	H	I
1	Days	3/4/2012	3/5/2012	3/6/2012	3/7/2012	3/8/2012	3/9/2012	3/10/2012	3/11/2012
2	Moe [Labor]	0.0	2.0	2.0	2.0	1.5	1.0	0.0	0.0
3	Total	0.0	2.0	2.0	2.0	1.5	1.0	0.0	0.0

(c)

FIGURE 7.23
Total Hours (a), Regular Hours (b), Overtime Hours (c) resource report.

	A	B	C	D	E	F	G	H
1	Days	3/4/2012	3/5/2012	3/6/2012	3/7/2012	3/8/2012	3/9/2012	3/10/2012
2	Task 1	0.000	0.781	0.938	0.990	1.001	0.997	0.000
3	Total							

FIGURE 7.24
Task schedule pressure.

by looking at the Task Total Cost report. We can add an additional management rule to our default management policy that reduces the number of OT hours as costs begin to escalate. Open up the Mgmt Policies view, and select the Default management policy. Next, select the rule "Overtime Policy from CPI." This rule seeks to reduce the assignment of OT hours as costs escalate. Figure 7.25 shows the policy that we will put into place. This policy says to reduce the OT hours that are requested by 3.0 when cost pressure is between 0.0 and 0.10. As the cost pressure decreases, so too does the desire to reduce the OT hours that are worked. Once the cost pressure is 0.9 or greater, management will not try to reduce any of the OT hours.

Before rerunning the simulation with this new policy, we need to make a change to the project-level settings. In the Project Settings dialog, there is an option to set a balance between the schedule and cost pressure policies (Figure 7.26). Because the cost and schedule pressure policies work to

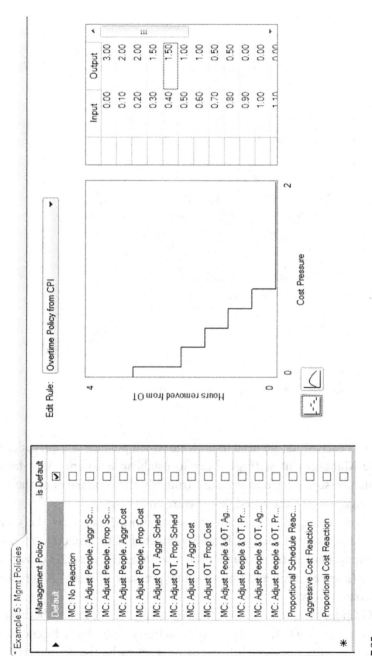

FIGURE 7.25
Overtime policy from cost pressure.

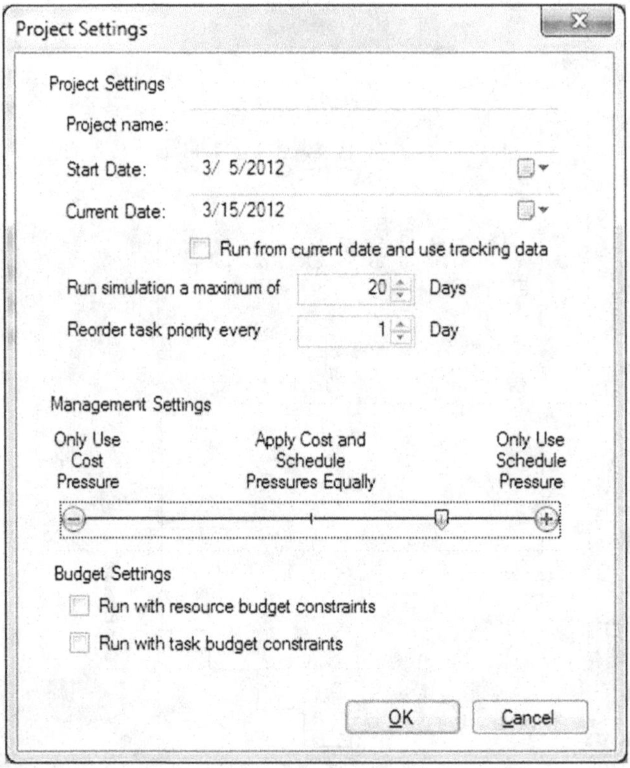

FIGURE 7.26
Setting the cost-versus-schedule pressure trade-off rule.

counteract each other, we need to indicate which policies take precedence. Use the Management settings slider to establish a balance that favors schedule pressure over cost pressure (roughly three-quarters of the way on the slider toward the schedule-pressure end of the scale.

Save your changes, and rerun the simulation. First, view the Gantt chart, and notice that the task is now completed at 10 a.m. on the following Monday. Look at the resource overtime hours (Figure 7.27a), task cost pressure (Figure 7.27b), and task schedule pressure (Figure 7.27c) reports to understand why.

The OT hours worked are lower than in the previous example because as Moe starts working OT, he drives up the actual cost of the task generating cost pressure. Because schedule pressure is set to be the primary policy driver, the OT hours worked are still sufficient to complete the task earlier than when no OT was requested, but it took longer than the case where

(a)

	A	B	C	D	E	F	G	H	I	J	K
1	Days	3/4/2012	3/5/2012	3/6/2012	3/7/2012	3/8/2012	3/9/2012	3/10/2012	3/11/2012	3/12/2012	3/13/2012
2	Moe [Labor]	0.0	2.0	2.0	1.8	0.8	0.9	0.1	0.0	0.0	0.0
3	Total	0.0	2.0	2.0	1.8	0.8	0.9	0.1	0.0	0.0	0.0

(b)

	A	B	C	D	E	F	G	H	I	J	K
1	Days	3/4/2012	3/5/2012	3/6/2012	3/7/2012	3/8/2012	3/9/2012	3/10/2012	3/11/2012	3/12/2012	3/13/2012
2	Task 1	0.000	0.568	0.682	0.721	0.747	0.763	0.762	0.762	0.751	0.000
3	Total										

(c)

	A	B	C	D	E	F	G	H	I	J	K
1	Days	3/4/2012	3/5/2012	3/6/2012	3/7/2012	3/8/2012	3/9/2012	3/10/2012	3/11/2012	3/12/2012	3/13/2012
2	Task 1	0.000	0.781	0.938	0.981	0.976	0.975	0.977	0.977	1.000	0.000
3	Total										

FIGURE 7.27

Resource overtime hours (a), task cost pressure (b), task schedule pressure (c).

	Low productivity, no action (baseline)	Allow overtime	Allow overtime, cost constrained
Start day, hour	3/5/12 8:00 a.m.	3/5/12 8:00 a.m.	3/5/12 8:00 a.m.
End day, hour	3/13/12 11:00 a.m.	3/9/12 6:00 p.m.	3/12/12 10:00 a.m.
Total regular hours	51.0	40.0	42.0
Total overtime hours	0.0	8.4	7.5
Total cost	$510.00	$527.00	$532.00

FIGURE 7.28
Comparison of management policies.

there was no concern for cost pressure. Figure 7.28 summarizes the results for three cases:

1. Low productivity without management intervention
2. Management actions allowing OT
3. Management actions allowing OT, tempered by cost pressure

In the table are the start and end times for Task 1, the total regular and OT hours worked, and the total cost to complete the task. Looking at the end times for the task, the results are as expected. The task allowed to work the most OT finished closest to the expected end time of 3/9/12 at 5:00 p.m. The task constrained by cost pressure finished the following Monday at 10:00 a.m., while the baseline took an additional day's worth of work to complete. What is less obvious is that the OT-only policy actually resulted in a slightly cheaper task. This seems counterintuitive until you realize that this occurs because in the cost-constrained case, Moe ended up working on the task a second Monday when he is at his least productive. These results show how management policies need to be applied wisely in response to the other project constraints in order to be most effective.

DPM VERSUS CPM

One of the key tenets of the DPM philosophy is to model the project as realistically as possible. Traditional CPM tools offer tools like resource level loading but fail to account for the realities of variable productivity, OT, and resource constraints as a counter to desired management policies.

EXAMPLE 6—MULTIPLE TASK RESOURCES

Our next example examines the application of multiple resources that are assigned to a task. It explores the conditions under which it makes sense to aggregate resources and when to divide tasks into related subtasks. For this example, start a new project, adding a single task (e.g., "Task 1") and a labor resource (e.g., "Moe" with a work scope of 40 h). Next, we will add a piece of equipment that is required for Moe to complete his work. Instead of defining the equipment from the Gantt view, however, we will define the equipment in the Resource view so that all of its attributes can be set at once. Open up the Resource view. Add a new resource by typing in its name in the row beneath Moe. Tab over to set the resource type by clicking the cell, displaying a drop-down list and selecting "Equipment," or simply typing the letter "E." Next, update the hourly cost for the equipment, for example, $100.00. In the OT rate multiplier, change the default from 1.5 to 1.0 indicating that there is no added cost for operating the equipment. Lastly, tab to the Calendar cell, and select the "24 Hour" calendar indicating that the equipment is available 24/7. Once entered, your resource view should look similar to the one that is shown in Figure 7.29.

Next, we want to indicate that Task 1 uses the equipment "Machine." Return to the Gantt view if you have not already done so. This time, instead of typing in the resource name, either double-click in Task 1's Resource grid cell or right-click, accessing the context menu, then select "Edit Resources." A dialog like the one shown in Figure 7.30 appears.

Use this dialog to select the resources that a task requires. In the above example, we will use both of the defined resources: Moe and Machine. Moe is already associated with the task and needs no additional edits. Add "Machine" to the task by checking the "Use" option next to the resource's name. Enter a work scope of 20 h along with a 1.0 unit. Click "OK," and run the simulation. In the Gantt view, you will see that Task 1 starts at 12:00 a.m. the first day of the simulation, while the task finishes at 5:00 p.m. five days later. In this instance, each resource independently completes its required work. Because the machine uses the 24-h calendar, it completes its entire 20 h of work the first day of the project, while Moe works down his backlog at a rate of 8 h/day. View the Resource Regular Hours report (Figure 7.31) to confirm that this is indeed what happened.

We can model the requirement that Moe be present in order for the machine to operate by indicating that he is a required resource. Open up

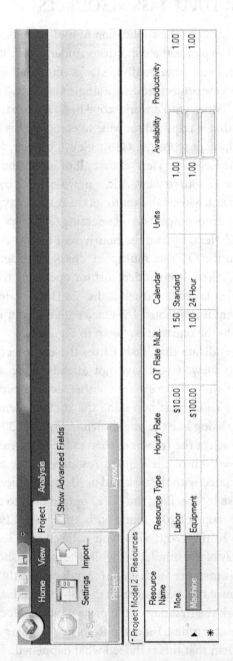

FIGURE 7.29
Defining an equipment resource.

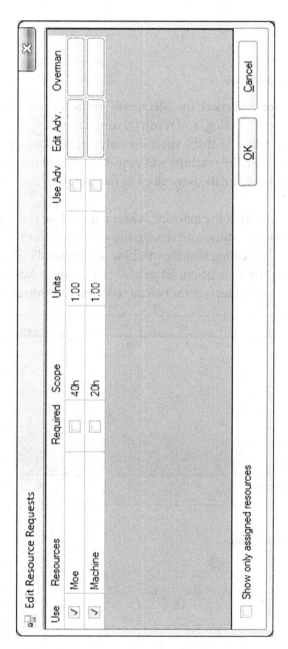

FIGURE 7.30
Edit Task Resource dialog.

	A	B	C	D	E	F	G	H
1	Days	3/4/2012	3/5/2012	3/6/2012	3/7/2012	3/8/2012	3/9/2012	3/10/2012
2	Machine [Equipment]	0.0	20.0	0.0	0.0	0.0	0.0	0.0
3	Moe [Labor]	0.0	8.0	8.0	8.0	8.0	8.0	0.0
4	Total	0.0	28.0	8.0	8.0	8.0	8.0	0.0

FIGURE 7.31
Regular hours worked by resource.

the Resource editor, and check the "Required" option next to Moe's name (Figure 7.32), close the dialog, and rerun the simulation.

The results now show that the machine only operated when Moe was also working. Because the machine was required for only the first half of the task (20 h versus 40 h), its usage stops in the middle of the third workday (Figure 7.33).

Let us now assume that the machine is also required for the entire task. Open up the Resource editor, and change the work scope for the machine from 20 h to 40 h indicating that the machine is "Required" (Figure 7.34).

Before running the simulation, let us also change the machine's availability so that it is out of service for two days during the project. Go to the

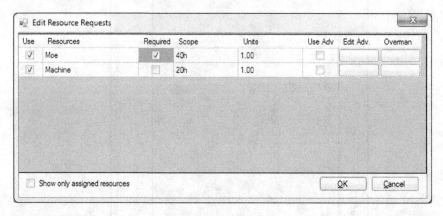

FIGURE 7.32
Identifying a required resource.

	A	B	C	D	E	F	G	H
1	Days	3/4/2012	3/5/2012	3/6/2012	3/7/2012	3/8/2012	3/9/2012	3/10/2012
2	Machine [Equipment]	0.0	8.0	8.0	4.0	0.0	0.0	0.0
3	Moe [Labor]	0.0	8.0	8.0	8.0	8.0	8.0	0.0
4	Total	0.0	16.0	16.0	12.0	8.0	8.0	0.0

FIGURE 7.33
Impact of a required resource.

FIGURE 7.34
Editing machine requirements.

resource view, and click in the "Availability" cell for Machine to display the schedule editor. Select the "Work Exceptions" tab, and then on days 3/8 and 3/9, click on all of the hours so that the machine is not available on those days (Figure 7.35).

Run the simulation. The Gantt view shows that the task now takes two additional days to complete. Because Moe needed the machine to complete his work, he accomplished no work when the machine was out of service. This is quite a different behavior from the previous example where Moe only needed the machine for half of the task. Figure 7.36 shows the

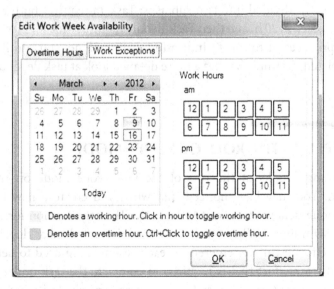

FIGURE 7.35
Editing machine availability.

	A	B	C	D	E	F	G	H	I	J	K	L
1	Days	3/4/2012	3/5/2012	3/6/2012	3/7/2012	3/8/2012	3/9/2012	3/10/2012	3/11/2012	3/12/2012	3/13/2012	3/14/2012
2	Machine [Equipment]	0.0	8.0	8.0	8.0	0.0	0.0	0.0	0.0	8.0	8.0	0.0
3	Moe [Labor]	0.0	8.0	8.0	8.0	0.0	0.0	0.0	0.0	8.0	8.0	0.0
4	Total	0.0	16.0	16.0	16.0	0.0	0.0	0.0	0.0	16.0	16.0	0.0

FIGURE 7.36
Machine and Moe work hours when machine has downtime.

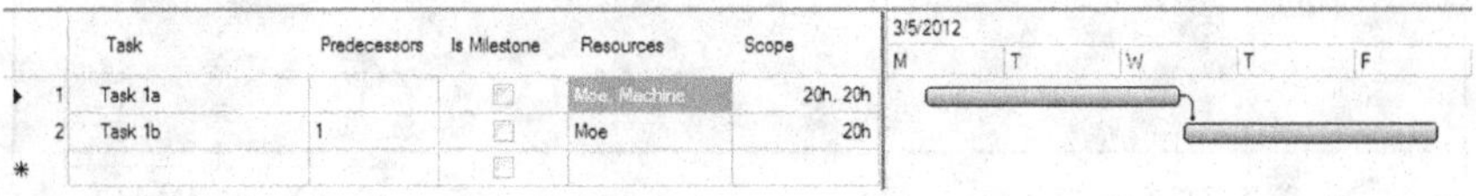

FIGURE 7.37
Using subtasks to model complex resource constraints.

hours that are worked by day. It shows that when the machine is not available, no work is accomplished.

There is one important behavior to note for required resources. Once a required resource completes its work scope, it no longer factors into the work progress evaluation. For example, if the machine was marked as required but only had a work scope of 20 h, once those 20 h are completed, Moe completes his remaining hours of work without using the equipment. If two or more resources are required for a task, it is best to create one task where each required resource has the same work scope and then add a second task for the remaining scope. Figure 7.37 shows an example of this. Task 1 is divided into two subtasks: Task 1a requires both Moe and Machine, each at 20 h, and then Task 1b only requires Moe for 20 h. Task 1b sets its predecessor to row #1 indicating that it will not start until Task 1a is completed. Example 8 takes a more detailed look at task dependencies.

EXAMPLE 7—THE ROLE OF SCOPE MODE

This example looks at the role of the task scope mode on the project plan. You may have noticed that when you create a new task, the scope mode defaults to "TreatAsBacklog." The other option for a task is "TreatAsDuration." When a task scope mode is treated as backlog, it means that the effort estimates entered for each resource are used to determine the total work effort that is required to complete the task under normal work conditions (e.g., no variations in worker productivity, no resource constraints). The DPM uses scope as backlog as the default because the expectation is that task durations are not known a priori but can only be determined as resources perform work (Figure 7.38). Use TreatAsDuration when you wish to specify a task with a known duration, and expect that there will be little-to-no impact due to resource productivity and availability. That said, pmBLOX still enforces resource constraints on tasks that are marked as duration tasks when named resources are assigned to the task. To see how the TreatAsDuration mode operates, start a new project, and define a single task, Task 1, that uses TreatAsDuration as its scope mode. Also, enter the work scope to be 5d (five days).

As expected, the task takes five days to complete. Next, enter in a resource name, for example, "Larry," and set the scope to 5d again. Rerunning the simulation, you will see no change in the total task duration. Open the Resource editor for Task 1, and change the number of resources that are required from 1.0 to 0.5. Essentially, this says that Larry works half time on Task 1 (Figure 7.39). Rerun the simulation, and the task is still completed in five days.

Note: When scope is used to calculate task duration, the task is expected to take the longest period of time for any resources that are assigned to the task. If we added Curly as a resource to Task 1 and set his scope to 8 days, Task 1 would now take eight days to complete.

To see the difference between scope as backlog and scope as duration, change Task 1 from "TreatAsDuration" to "TreatAsBacklog," and rerun

FIGURE 7.38
Task operating under TreatAsDuration rules.

FIGURE 7.39
Setting a resource to half time.

FIGURE 7.40
Using TreatAsBacklog on a task worked half time.

the simulation (Figure 7.40). The task now takes 10 workdays to complete because Larry is only working 4 h a day but still has 40 h of work to complete.

Set Task 1 back to "TreatAsDuration," and double-click on "Larry" to open the resource editor. Change the number of units required from 0.5 to 2.0. Save your changes, and rerun the simulation. Notice that the task now takes 10 workdays, not the 5 that is specified. Because there is only one Larry available, but two were expected to fulfill the task duration, the DPM treats this as a resource constraint that cannot be ignored.

Note: If you want to define a task that is a true fixed duration, either set the duration without naming any resources or ensure that there are sufficient resources that are defined to fulfill the resource request.

EXAMPLE 8—TASK DEPENDENCIES

Projects consist of multiple tasks, with dependencies between tasks. pmBLOX lets you set dependency relationships by establishing the predecessor tasks in the Gantt view. You define predecessors by entering in the row ID of the preceding tasks in the "Predecessors" cell. You can enter more than one dependency by typing in the numbers that are separated by commas. Figure 7.41 shows an example where three tasks (Task 1, Task 2, and Task 3) are defined with Task 2 depending on Task 1 and Task 3 depending on Tasks 1 and 2.

	Task	Predecessors	Is Milestone	Resources	Scope	Scope Mode	March 26 4	11
1	Task 1		☐	Moe		20h TreatAsBacklog		
2	Task 2	1	☐	Larry		20h TreatAsBacklog		
3	Task 3	1,2	☐	Moe		20h TreatAsBacklog		
*			☐					

FIGURE 7.41
Defining multiple tasks.

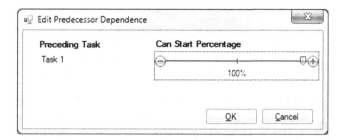

FIGURE 7.42
Task 2 predecessor dependency rule.

Traditional CPM-based tools use concepts like start-to-finish or start-to-start along with lag and lead times to establish rules governing task dependencies. The DPM uses an approach that is tied to task completion rates. Because task completion rates are by nature dynamic, it does not make sense to talk simply in terms of fixed lag or lead times. Instead, the DPM defines dependencies relative to the progress of the preceding tasks. By default in pmBLOX, tasks that have predecessors will start once the predecessor tasks are 100% complete. This amounts to a start-to-finish relationship in CPM project plans. You can change this dependency by either double-clicking in the Predecessor field or right-clicking in a Gantt view row and then selecting the "Edit Predecessors" option. Figure 7.42 shows an example of the predecessor editor.

Setting the percentage for a predecessor task to 100% is equivalent to establishing a start-to-finish relationship. A percentage set to 0% is equivalent to a start-to-start relationship. Other than these two cases, the DPM rules for establishing predecessor–successor relationships do not map directly to CPM-based methods.

DPM VERSUS CPM

If you are trying to mirror a CPM project in pmBLOX, you can approximate the percentages by determining a percent for the lag time relative to the predecessor task duration. For example, if a CPM plan has a 5-day task with a lag time of −2 days, that would be equivalent to setting the predecessor relationship to 60%. Calculate the percent of the task that lags, in this case 2 days divided by 5 days, or 40% of the tasks. Subtracting that percent from 100% (task complete) results in a 60% dependency.

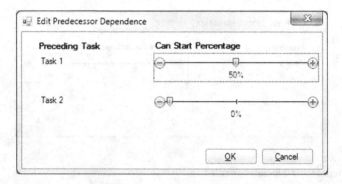

FIGURE 7.43
Task 3 predecessor dependency rules.

For this example, set the relationship between Task 2 and its predecessor, Task 1, to 50%. Similarly, set the percentages for Task 3 to 50% for Task 1 and 0% for Task 2 (Figure 7.43).

Once set, rerun your simulation. As expected, Task 2 starts when Task 1 is halfway through its work scope. Task 3 does not start until Task 1 is 100% complete even though the dependency rule says that it can start as soon as Task 1 is 50% complete. The reason Task 3 does not start sooner is how pmBLOX assigns resources to tasks. Even though Task 3 could potentially start, Moe is already working on Task 1 and does so until he completes the task (Figure 7.44).

Task start times and resource assignments are determined using a sophisticated algorithm that evaluates five criteria within the simulation:

1. Task start constraints
2. Task priority
3. Task schedule pressure
4. Resource requirements
5. Project rescheduling frequency

Each task can exist in one of several distinct states: Not Started, Can Start, Started, and Finished. A task is initially in the "Not Started" state and

	Task	Predecessors	Is Milestone	Resources	Scope	3/5/2012 M	T	W	T	F
1	Task 1			Moe	20h					
2	Task 2	1		Larry	20h					
3	Task 3	1,2		Moe	20h					
*										

FIGURE 7.44
Task predecessor–successor results.

only moves to the "Can Start" state when its start constraints are satisfied. Once a task reaches the "Can Start" state, it is able to request resources and perform work. The "Can Start" state also starts the tracking of expected versus actual work accomplishment, potentially resulting in schedule pressure within the task. Once a task sees work performed, it moves to the "Started" state. Started tasks take precedence over "Can Start" tasks when assigning resources. Lastly, once all the task work completes, it is marked as "Finished." Once finished, the task no longer requests resources.

pmBLOX defines four distinct modes of behavior determining when a task can start:

1. As soon as possible
2. As soon as resource is available
3. Must start on
4. Start no earlier than

The "as soon as possible" constraint is the default behavior. In this mode, as soon as predecessor constraints are fulfilled, the task is in a "can start" state. The "as soon as resource is available" is a variation on the "as soon as possible" constraint in that it also accounts for resource availability. Using this constraint ensures that a task's "can start" state is only set once all predecessor requirements are fulfilled and all resources are available. The "must start on" constraint is when you require a task to start on a given date. Setting the "must start on" date does not guarantee that work will be performed—task predecessor dependencies and resource availability can still constrain actual work accomplishment. Lastly, the "start no earlier than" constraint can be used to ensure that a task does not start too early in the overall project. You use this constraint mode when you have a task that has no predecessor constraints, but you want to defer the actual start time.

Once a task achieves the "can start" state, it is able to request resources and perform work if the resources are available. Every task is assigned a relative priority on a scale of 1 (low) to 999 (high), with the default value being 500. This priority, combined with the task's schedule pressure, results in an adjusted priority. pmBLOX orders tasks by looking at their start state and adjusted priority. Resources are assigned to tasks based on this prioritized order. If a task has additional resource constraints that prevent it from working (e.g., a required resource is not available), it frees up any resources that are claimed, allowing other tasks that require the resource to perform their work.

In the real world, managers do not react on an hourly basis to perceived changes in task priority. pmBLOX reflects this reality by specifying the frequency with which tasks are reprioritized. The default is daily, but it often makes sense to adjust this value to 5 or 10 days for very long projects. You can modify the task reprioritization frequency from the Project Settings dialog.

In our previous example, all of the tasks had the same relative priority. Let us now examine what happens when the task priority changes. Return to your last example, set the priority of Task 3 to 600, and rerun your simulation. Figure 7.45 shows a markedly different project schedule when Task 3 has a higher priority.

Notice that Task 3 now starts as soon as Task 1 is 50% complete, exactly matching the task percent dependencies. Task 3's higher priority ensures that Moe is assigned once the predecessor constraints were satisfied. The Gantt chart itself does not fully explain where Moe is spending his time, however. To see that, go to the Reports view, and display the Task Report for Productive Hours. Figure 7.46 shows the hours worked on each of our three tasks. Looking at Tasks 1 and 3, the two tasks where Moe is assigned, we see the details of his workweek.

On the second day of the project, Moe switches gears from Task 1 to start work on Task 3 after completing just over 50% of the Task 1 work. This is because Task 3's higher priority gives it the first opportunity to claim the resource. Once assigned to Task 3, Moe works full time on Task 3 day 3. However, by day 4, Moe returns to Task 1. This happens

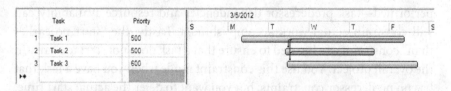

	Task	Priority
1	Task 1	500
2	Task 2	500
3	Task 3	600

FIGURE 7.45
Influence of priority on task progress.

	A	B	C	D	E	F	G	H
1	Days	3/4/2012	3/5/2012	3/6/2012	3/7/2012	3/8/2012	3/9/2012	3/10/2012
2	Task 1	0.0	8.0	3.0	0.0	8.0	1.0	0.0
3	Task 2	0.0	0.0	6.0	8.0	6.0	0.0	0.0
4	Task 3	0.0	0.0	5.0	8.0	0.0	7.0	0.0
5	Total							

FIGURE 7.46
Productive work hours for tasks.

DPM VERSUS CPM

In traditional CPM tools, the dependency rules will typically override any resource constraints. In those tools, it may indicate that a resource is overallocated, but the baseline project schedule ignores that fact. Only if you try to level load resources will the impact of overallocating resources surface. In contrast, the DPM always treats resource constraints as the primary driver for task durations. This ensures that project plans realistically represent task durations given the project's resources.

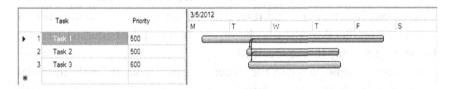

FIGURE 7.47
Adjusting task reprioritization alters project outcome.

because the mounting schedule pressure on Task 1 results in a shifting priority for Moe. Moe finishes Task 1 on the morning of the fifth day and then goes on to complete Task 3.

Lastly, let us look at the impact that changing task reprioritization has on project outcome. Open up the "Project Settings" dialog, change the "Reorder task priority" to two days, save the change, and rerun the simulation. Figure 7.47 shows a markedly different schedule resulting from the changed task reprioritization frequency. In this case, Moe ends up completing his 20 h of work on Task 3 before returning to Task 1.

EXAMPLE 9—WORKING WITH MATERIALS

Our last example looks at how you can use material resources in pmBLOX. Materials differ from labor and equipment resources in two ways. Firstly, materials are a consumable resource—once used, they cannot be reused. Secondly, materials have no direct impact on work that is accomplished but serve as an additional constraint on whether or not work can proceed. If materials are required but are not available, work on a task stops.

The user defines materials in one of two ways. Firstly, using the resource view, you can define a materials inventory for your project. Secondly, you can have a project task produce materials resulting from task accomplishment. We will look at each of these two cases independently.

Start a new project, and define a single task, Task 1, with Moe performing 40 h of work on this task. Next, switch to the Resource view (Figure 7.48).

You define a material by providing a unique name, an initial inventory, and a unit cost. The initial inventory represents the quantity of the material at the start of the project. You can also use the Delivery Schedule dialog (Figure 7.49) to change the materials inventory over the course of the simulation. Select a date, and then enter in the number of materials that will arrive on that day. The simulation assumes that the materials arrive at the start of the day that is specified.

For this example, enter in the material name "Widget" with an initial quantity of 1. Once entered, return to the Gantt view. For Task 1, scroll

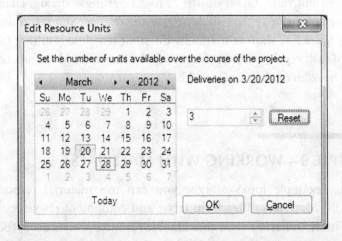

FIGURE 7.48
Defining a material resource.

FIGURE 7.49
Defining a material delivery schedule.

over to the column titled "Materials Req'd." Either double-click in this cell or right-click on the task row, and select "Edit Materials" from the context menu. Either action displays a dialog like the one that is shown in Figure 7.50.

On this dialog, you select the material that is required to complete the task, the number of materials that are required and when the material is required. For this example, select "Widget," set the quantity required to "1," and set the percent complete to "0." This percentage means that the material is required to start the task (Figure 7.51). Run the simulation. The Gantt view shows a task completing in five days, as expected. Now, return to the resource view and change the initial quantity on hand to 0, and set a delivery schedule so that 1 unit of material arrives on 3/8. (Our example project's start date was set to 3/5.)

Save the changes, and rerun the simulation. You will see that the task does not start until 3/8 because of the delayed material availability.

You can configure materials to be required at different times during a task as well. In the Gantt view, edit the materials so that we require one widget at the start of the task and another widget when the task is 50% complete (Figure 7.52).

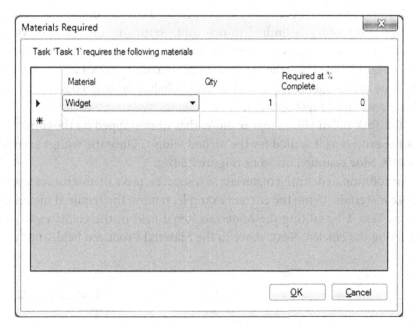

FIGURE 7.50
Assigning materials to a task.

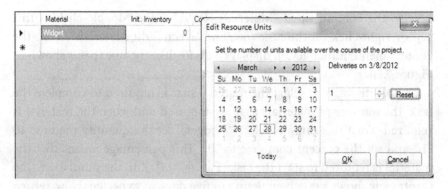

FIGURE 7.51
Changing material availability and delivery schedule.

Task 'Task 1' requires the following materials		
Material	Qty	Required at % Complete
▶ Widget ▾	1	0
Widget	1	50
✳		

FIGURE 7.52
Setting a required materials schedule.

If you try to run the simulation now, Task 1 is never completed because material inventory is limited to one unit. Return to the resource view, and change the initial inventory back to one unit and rerun the simulation. Figure 7.53 shows the outcome of this scenario. Task 1 starts on time because one widget is available, but work is halted for half a day as we wait for the second widget delivery.

The Task Billed Hours report shows that work stopped on the third day of the project as it waited for the second widget. Once the widget arrived on 3/8, Moe resumed his work (Figure 7.54).

In addition to defining materials as resources, tasks themselves can produce materials. Using the current example, remove the required materials from Task 1 by editing the Materials Req'd field in the Gantt view and deleting the entries. Next, move to the Material Produced field, and type

	Task	Start	Finish	% Complete	March	
					4	11
▶ 1	Task 1	3/5/2012 8:00 AM	3/12/2012 12:00 PM	100.00		
✳						

FIGURE 7.53
Task delayed waiting for material.

	A	B	C	D	E	F	G	H	I	J	K
1	Days	3/4/2012	3/5/2012	3/6/2012	3/7/2012	3/8/2012	3/9/2012	3/10/2012	3/11/2012	3/12/2012	3/13/2012
2	Task 1	0.0	8.0	8.0	4.0	8.0	8.0	0.0	0.0	4.0	0.0
3	Total										

FIGURE 7.54

Work rate waiting for material.

	Task	Scope	Materials Req'd	Matl's Req'd Qty	Matl's Req'd at %	Material Produced	Qty Produced	Matl Produced at %
1	Task 1	40h				Gizmo	1	100
2	Task 2	40h	Gizmo	1		0		

FIGURE 7.55

Defining a task that produces a material.

in "Gizmo." Once added, the quantity produced shows "1," and it shows that the gizmo is available when the task finishes. Next, insert a second task, named "Task 2," assigning 40 h of work to "Larry." Set up Task 2 to require one gizmo at the start of the task, as shown in Figure 7.55.

Run the simulation. Notice that Task 2 does not start until Task 1 completes even though there was no predecessor relationship that is set between the two tasks. In this example, the material requirement acts similarly to a traditional predecessor relationship.

FINAL COMMENTS

In this chapter, you learned how to create project files in pmBLOX and define tasks, resources, and the relationship between tasks and resources. Basic examples highlighted how the DPM performs planning calculations and differentiated the approach from traditional CPM-based planning tools. With the basics learned in this chapter, you can begin to apply the DPM to your project management tasks. Yet, we have just scratched the surface of both the DPM methodology and pmBLOX's advanced project planning features. Other example files and additional content can be found at http://www.pmblox.com and http://www.dynamicprogressmethod.com. In Chapter 8, we will explore a more advanced analysis capability that is available with the DPM: project acceleration.

8

---

*Advanced Capabilities
of Dynamic Progress Method*

INTRODUCTION

Chapter 7 introduced the user interface and functionality for pmBLOX®
(Dynamic Progress Method [DPM]–based project planning tool) and
showed how to build a very simple project. This chapter works with a more
complicated example project to show some of the advanced analysis capabilities of the DPM approach.

EXAMPLE MICROSOFT PROJECT FILE

The basis for this example is one of the project plans that was used in
the Defense Advanced Research Project Agency (DARPA) Small Business
Innovation Research (SBIR) project that was described in Chapter 1
(which is available on http://www.dynamicprogressmethod.com as well as
http://www.pmblox.com). It is the implementation project for a finance
and accounting system for a large commercial organization. The exact
details of the project are not necessary, but the magnitude of the project is
worth discussing. Figure 8.1 shows the top portion of the project, as shown
in Microsoft Project 2013. Figure 8.2 shows the bottom portion of the project, as shown in Microsoft Project 2013, to indicate that the project has a
combination of 138 tasks and milestones and occurs over a time frame

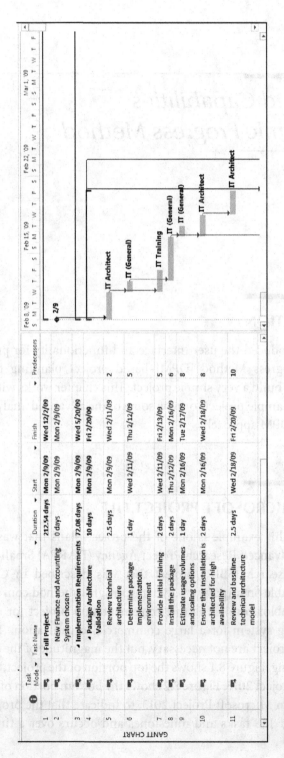

FIGURE 8.1

Microsoft Project example (top portion).

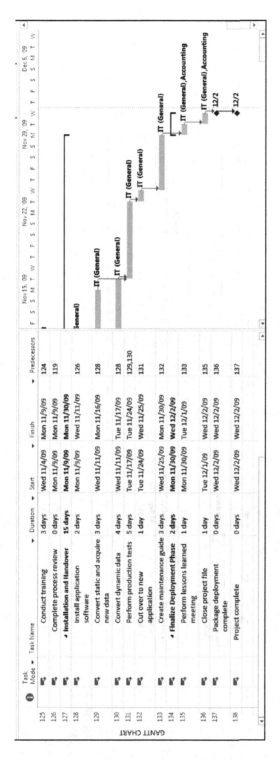

FIGURE 8.2

Microsoft Project example (bottom portion).

FIGURE 8.3

Major phases of example project.

of about 10 months. While there are certainly more complicated projects than this, this project is of sufficient size to demonstrate the value of DPM for project planning and management. Figure 8.3 shows the *collapsed* view of the major project phases:

- Implementation requirements
- Package integration design
- Package integration
- Package deployment

Table 8.1 provides details on the resources that were used in the project. It shows the number of personnel in the Units column (e.g., 100% equals one person; 200% equals two people), the standard hourly rate for that resource, and the overtime (OT) rate for that resource (if needed). The final column on the right is a factor that will be used in pmBLOX, the OT multiplier, which is a multiplier on the standard hourly rate for any hour that the resource is used for OT work. An OT multiplier of 1.00 indicates that the standard hourly rate and the OT hourly rate are the exact same.

Table 8.2 shows a summary of the start and end dates, durations, and costs for each of the four major phases, along with the entire project. The project starts on 2/9/2009 and ends on 12/2/2009 with a duration of 296 calendar days at a cost of $288,867, according to Microsoft Project. The first major phase of the project, implementation requirements, starts on 2/9/2009 and ends on 5/20/2009 with a duration of 100 calendar days and a cost of $73,860.

TABLE 8.1

Resource Information for Example Project

Resource Name	Units	Standard Rate	OT Rate	OT Mult
Accounting	100%	$115.00	$125.00	1.09
Business analysts	100%	$95.00	$115.00	1.21
Executive management	100%	$450.00	$450.00	1.00
IT (general)	200%	$75.00	$90.00	1.20
IT admins	200%	$80.00	$90.00	1.13
IT architect	100%	$150.00	$150.00	1.00
IT development	300%	$90.00	$105.00	1.17
IT testing	300%	$60.00	$75.00	1.25
IT training	100%	$70.00	$80.00	1.14
Legal	100%	$225.00	$225.00	1.00
Purchasing	100%	$50.00	$65.00	1.30

TABLE 8.2

Summary Outputs for Example Project (in Microsoft Project)

Phase	Version: Microsoft Project			
	Start	End	Duration	Cost
Implementation requirements	2/9/2009	5/20/2009	100	$73,860
Package integration design	5/20/2009	8/11/2009	83	$69,127
Package integration	7/7/2009	10/14/2009	99	$98,040
Package deployment	10/14/2009	12/2/2009	49	$47,840
Total	2/9/2009	12/2/2009	296	$288,867

IMPORTING A MICROSOFT PROJECT XML FILE INTO pmBLOX

Files from Microsoft Project are imported into pmBLOX as XML files. Thus, before closing Microsoft Project, the user must choose Save As and select the XML format as the desired file format. Once in XML format, this file can be imported into pmBLOX. Figure 8.4 shows how to import an XML file. After opening a new pmBLOX project file, select Import in the top menu, as shown in the diagram. Then, select the appropriate XML file from your computer, as shown in Figure 8.5.

After selecting the XML file to import, the user will see a dialog box to confirm the import (Figure 8.6). After clicking OK to import the file, the user will see the option for mapping custom fields (Figure 8.7). Many of the variables used in pmBLOX are typically not available in Microsoft Project. This dialog box allows the user to map variables in the Microsoft Project file with pmBLOX variables. For example, one of the default selections is to map the field Task Budget in Microsoft Project to Budget (Task) in pmBLOX. At this point, simply click OK to accept all the default variable assignments.

After mapping the fields, the user will be given the option to run a simulation (Figure 8.8). Because pmBLOX is a simulation-based tool, any updates to the file are not made effective until a simulation is run. Microsoft Project, on the other hand, immediately updates values because it uses a spreadsheet approach instead of an operational simulation like pmBLOX (see Chapter 5 for more details on the two modeling technologies). Thus, no results will be seen with the import until a simulation is run. Another way to run the simulation is to click on the blue arrow in the Simulation Controller, as shown in Figure 8.9.

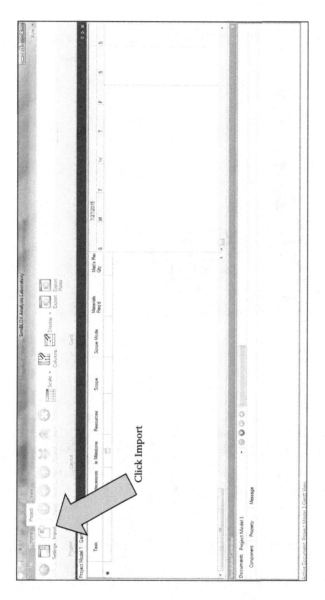

FIGURE 8.4

Importing a Microsoft Project XML file into pmBLOX.

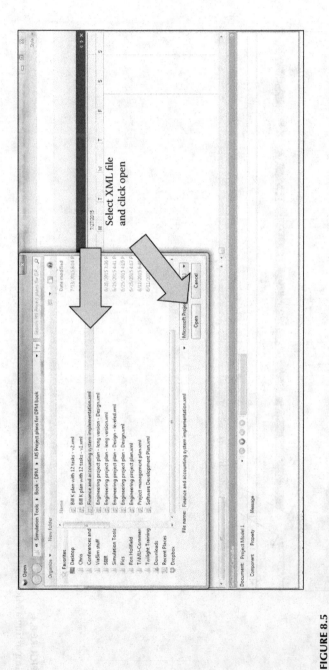

FIGURE 8.5

Selecting a Microsoft Project XML file to import into pmBLOX.

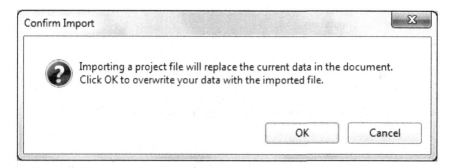

FIGURE 8.6
Confirm import of XML file.

FIGURE 8.7
Mapping custom fields.

Once the simulation for this project is run in pmBLOX, the results can be seen (Figure 8.10). Table 8.3 shows the results in the same table form as the Microsoft Project results in Table 8.2.

By comparing results from Tables 8.1 and 8.2, notice that pmBLOX suggests that the project can be completed slightly faster (284 days) than what Microsoft Project suggests (296 days). In some cases, pmBLOX (using the resource-based DPM approach) shows that the project will take longer than the duration that is suggested by Microsoft Project. This is typically due to the fact that Microsoft Project allows for the overallocation of resources, and, in many cases, Microsoft Project cannot solve for this

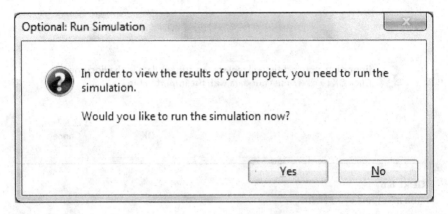

FIGURE 8.8
Run simulation.

overallocation with its resource leveling algorithms. However, in some cases, pmBLOX shows that the project will take shorter than the duration that is suggested by Microsoft Project. This is typically due to the fact that Microsoft Project will only use a resource when that resource's availability matches the desired availability that is set for the task. For example, if a resource is supposed to be used 100% (8 h in a day) for a task, if that resource is not available for the full 8 h on a given day, Microsoft Project will skip over that resource and allow the resource to sit idle. So, in this example, if the resource was only available for 4 h (50% available units) on one day (because, perhaps, that resource was used on another task), then Microsoft Project will let that resource sit idle for 4 h instead of putting it to work (which is what the DPM will do).

ACCELERATING THE PROJECT

One of the key benefits of DPM is the more realistic cost and schedule estimates that the method provides (compared to the CPM) because of the operational simulation of the allocation of resources and work completion for each task. This is seen in the difference between the baseline Microsoft Project model (in Table 8.1) and the baseline pmBLOX model (in Table 8.2).

Yet, the power of the DPM approach is that we can now conduct a much more advanced analysis on the project. One of the most common questions

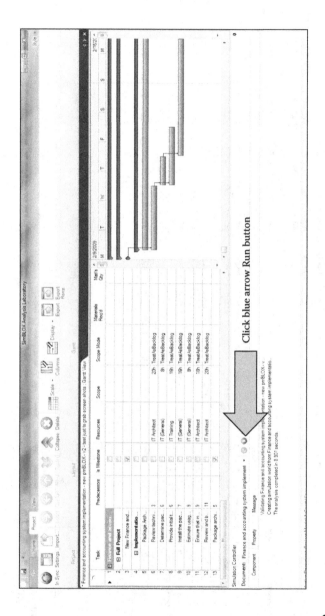

FIGURE 8.9

Run simulation (alternative approach).

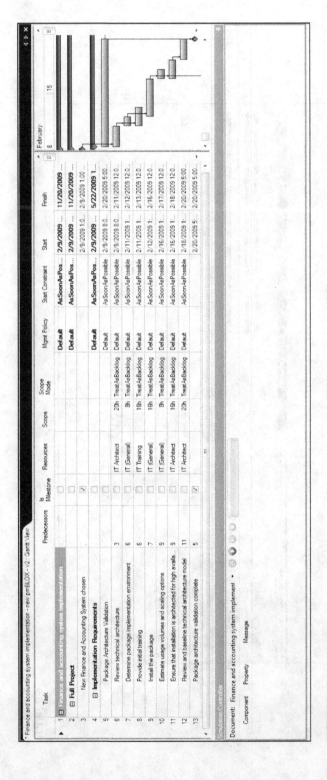

FIGURE 8.10
Results in pmBLOX.

TABLE 8.3

Summary Outputs for Example Project (in pmBLOX)

Phase	Version: pmBLOX Baseline (No Management Actions)			
	Start	**End**	**Duration**	**Cost**
Implementation requirements	2/9/2009	5/22/2009	102	$73,860
Package integration design	5/22/2009	8/27/2009	97	$69,127
Package integration	6/24/2009	9/30/2009	98	$98,040
Package deployment	9/30/2009	11/20/2009	51	$47,840
Total	2/9/2009	11/20/2009	284	$288,867

that is asked for any project is, "Can it be done faster?" As pointed out in Chapter 4 on the flaws of CPM, Microsoft Project cannot show the consequences of accelerating the project schedule. Microsoft Project (and any CPM-based tool) allows the user to set durations for any length, regardless of the logic or consistency of resource usage. Can a house be built in a day? Sure. Just set the duration equal to a day. There is no check on this assumption. Or, if we have a schedule that says that it takes 100 days to build a house, Microsoft Project allows the user to reduce this duration down to 1 day by using 100 times the resources (or a combination of lots of additional resources with everyone working 24 h a day). Without incorporating the negative effects of overtime (OT) fatigue and overmanning on resource productivity, CPM-based tools provide completely unrealistic project acceleration results, which lead to many project difficulties (e.g., rescheduling, shifting resources).

To incorporate some of the more realistic aspects of DPM, such as the negative impacts on resource productivity as seen in Figure 6.16, go to the Resources view in pmBLOX (see Chapter 7 for details on navigating pmBLOX), shown in Figure 8.11. For now, it is assumed that all resources have a *normal* productivity of 100% (1.00) on all tasks. This analysis could be made more interesting by making productivity changes among the resources. However, to limit the analysis in this chapter, all resources begin with 100% productivity. In Figure 8.11, notice that the number of resources of each type, the standard hourly rates, and the OT hourly rate multipliers (column heading of OT Rate Mult.) match those from the original Microsoft Project file in Table 8.1.

The first step that we need to do is to allow the resources to work some OT hours. By default, the Standard calendar in pmBLOX does not allow the resources to be available for OT work. For each of the resources, click

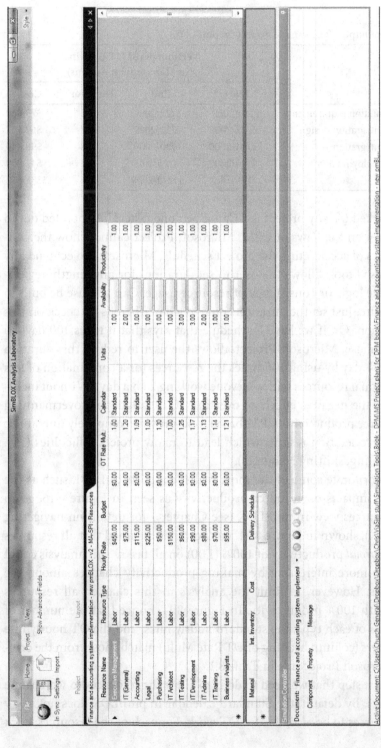

FIGURE 8.11

Resource view in pmBLOX.

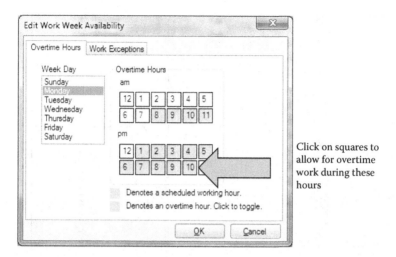

FIGURE 8.12
Six (6) h of OT allowed for resources.

on the Availability button, and set the availability of the resource to work 6 h of OT (Figure 8.12). *Note:* This does not mean that the resource automatically works these OT hours. This simply says that the resource is available to work these OT hours if the management policies or management actions require them to do so. For example, as shown in Figure 6.16, one management response to falling behind schedule is to increase the hours that are worked by the resources (i.e., add OT hours). To keep the analysis simple, this is the single management action that we will use for this project acceleration analysis.

We will need to use the Advanced Fields in the resource view of pmBLOX, so click on the checkbox for "Show Advanced Fields," as shown in Figure 8.13. This will open up additional input options for the resources (see right side of Figure 8.13). As stated, we will not be concerned with normal productivity in this analysis to keep it simple and keep the focus on the productivity impacts of working OT. Thus, we will not click on the Productivity button for any resource. Instead, click on the Fatigue button for a resource (far-right column in Figure 8.13).

Once you click on the Fatigue button for a resource, you will see the Fatigue Multiplier for the resource (Figure 8.14). The Fatigue Multiplier is a multiplier on the normal productivity level based on the Fatigue Index that is experienced by the resource. The Fatigue Index is a measure of the level of fatigue that is felt by the resource and is driven by the amount of OT that is worked by the resource. No fatigue accumulates if the resource

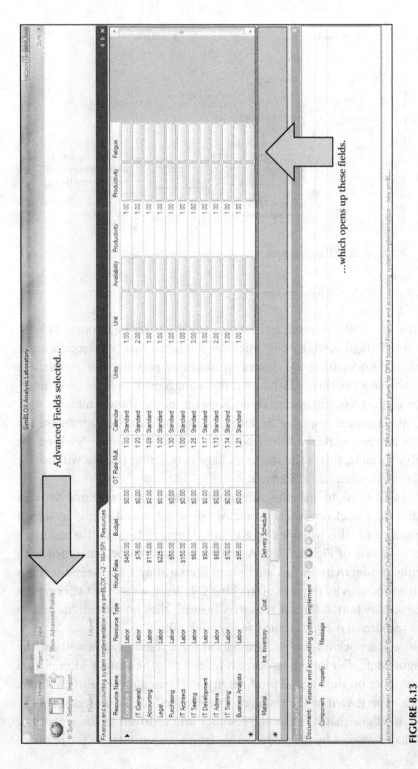

FIGURE 8.13
Select Advanced Fields to show additional options for resources in pmBLOX.

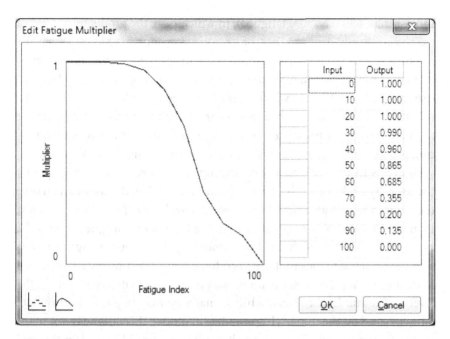

FIGURE 8.14
Default productivity impact of fatigue on resources.

is not working OT. Fatigue only accumulates when OT hours are worked. A Fatigue Index of 0 indicates that the resource has absolutely no fatigue and is *fresh*. At the other end, a Fatigue Index of 100 indicates that the resource is completely fatigued and cannot do work at all. Fatigue dissipates based on how fatigued the resource is. When the Fatigue Index is low (closer to 0), the resource recovers very quickly. In the real world, this is like working 2 h of OT on one day. The resource can come back to work the next day with very little or no impact of working the 2 h of OT the day before. Conversely, when a resource is very fatigued, the recovery rate is slower. Hence, when the Fatigue Index is high (closer to 100), the resource recovers very slowly. In the real world, this is like working 6 h of OT every day for four weeks in a row. When the resource comes back to work in the fifth week, even if it does not work OT, it is still feeling the effects of the previous four weeks of OT. Thus, in the fifth week, it is still not completely back to its normal productivity level. The resource must work a week or two without OT to get back to its normal productivity level.

By default, the values for the Fatigue Multiplier for all resources are those that are shown in Figure 8.14. Notice that by default, the resource does not begin to experience any productivity losses due to fatigue until the Fatigue

204 • The Dynamic Progress Method

Index reaches 30 (i.e., 30% fatigued), in which case, the productivity level of the resource only drops to 99% of its normal productivity level. When the resource is 40% fatigued, the resource only drops to 96% of its normal productivity level. There is a rapid drop until the resource is completely fatigued (Fatigue Index = 100), at which point the Fatigue Multiplier is 0, and the resource cannot do any work. This is a fairly conservative fatigue impact. The resource can experience quite a bit of fatigue before experiencing any significant productivity losses. This will be the curve that is used for this analysis.

Figures 8.15 and 8.16 show other examples of curves that can be input by the user. By clicking on the right column in the table, the user can change the values that are associated with the various levels of the Fatigue Index. Figure 8.15 shows a linear relationship: the level of the Fatigue Index is the exact productivity loss that is experienced by the resource. Figure 8.16 is a common set of values that are used for a nonhuman resource, such as a machine. Notice that there is no impact on productivity regardless of the level of Fatigue Index. Thus, while a machine may begin to accumulate fatigue based on the underlying simulation model, this fatigue is not manifested in the model. The end result is what we would expect in the real world. A machine can typically be run for a long time without a change in capability (until it breaks down, of course, or requires maintenance).

So far, we have set up the pmBLOX file so that the resources can work up to 6 h of OT on each workday (if needed), and we have established

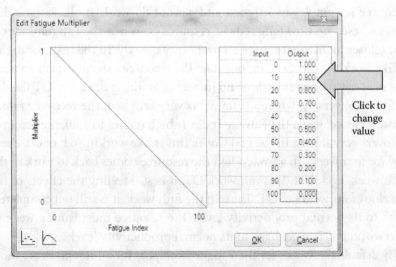

FIGURE 8.15
Example of linear impact of fatigue on resources.

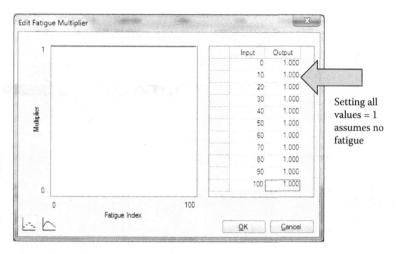

FIGURE 8.16
Example of no impact of fatigue on resources (e.g., Machine).

the productivity impacts of working OT and creating fatigue. Now, we need to add a management policy or management action that will be used to actually manage the project. With management actions, the DPM can show project managers whether or not their typical responses to project delays will help or hinder the project. As shown in Figure 8.17, go to the Management Action view in pmBLOX. The "Default" management policy will already be selected and applied to all tasks. *Note*: It will not be covered in detail in this book, but users can assign different policies to each task to represent the unique way in which certain tasks will be managed. Some details of management policies were provided in the "Example 5—Responding to Reduced Productivity" section in Chapter 7, particularly how to select the edit rule for "Overtime Policy for SPI."

"Overtime Policy for SPI" designates the number of OT hours that will be assigned (up to the maximum that a resource is available for working OT) for all the resources working on the task based on the schedule performance index (SPI; see Chapter 4 details of earned value). If the SPI < 1, the project is behind schedule and is running late. Figure 8.18 shows that the default values for OT hours are zero for all the values of the SPI. This means that no OT work will be assigned, regardless of how late or behind schedule the task is. For this acceleration analysis, set the values as seen in Figure 8.19. When the SPI drops from 1 (on schedule) to 0.9 (slightly behind schedule), the project manager will add 2 h of OT. (Remember, we set the availability of all resources to 6 h of OT each working day.) When the SPI

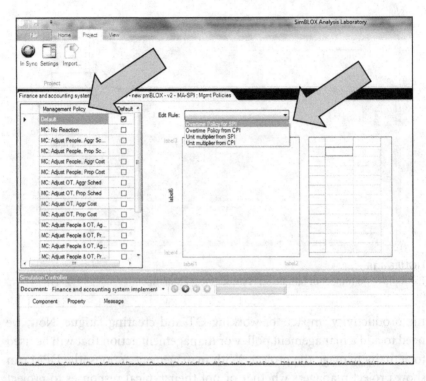

FIGURE 8.17
Default management actions for tasks.

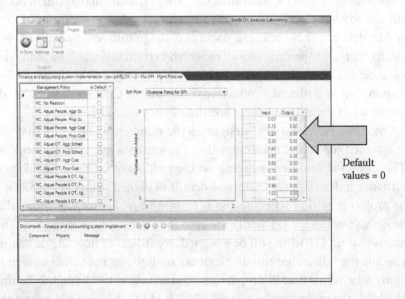

FIGURE 8.18
Default OT policy for SPI.

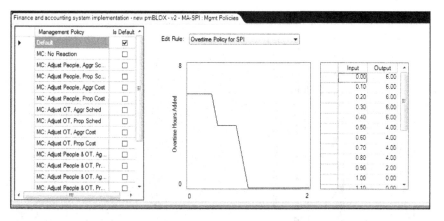

FIGURE 8.19
Change OT policy for SPI.

has a value of 0.5–0.8 (moderately behind schedule), the project manager will add 4 h of OT. Finally, when the SPI has a value that is less than 0.50 (severely behind schedule), the project manager will add 6 h of OT.

The resource adjustments have been made (i.e., available OT hours), the productivity impacts of fatigue have been included (i.e., Fatigue Multipliers), and a management policy has been implemented that only uses OT hours to try to make up schedule time if running late. We are now ready to accelerate the project and determine the trade-offs between schedule and cost. From the overview of the DPM model in Chapters 5 and 6, we know that there will be some cost impacts if we try to run the project faster, but now we will be able to quantify those trade-offs exactly for this example project.

To *accelerate* the project, in the Gantt view for the project, click on the Settings (Figure 8.20). At the bottom of the Settings dialog box are two multipliers: Planned Value Acceleration Multiplier (PV Mult) and Fatigue Adjustment. By default, these multipliers are set to 1.00 to indicate no changes (Figure 8.21). For this analysis, change the Fatigue Adjustment to 10. This is an appropriate level for the fatigue calculations in pmBLOX. Setting the Fatigue Adjustment to 10 is roughly equivalent to saying that a resource experiences 10% fatigue for an hour of OT. Keep in mind that the fatigue dissipates quickly when the resource is fresh. Thus, setting the Fatigue Adjustment to 10 is equivalent to saying that a resource could only work 24 h (a full day with 8 h of normal work and 16 h of OT work) before being completely fatigued. As long as the resource does not work 24 h solid, the resource recuperates and does not experience full fatigue.

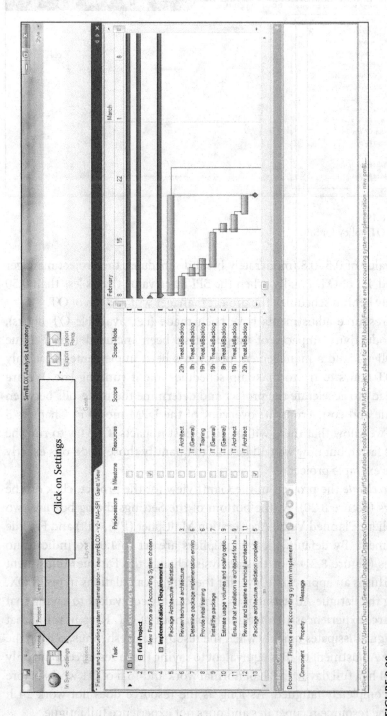

FIGURE 8.20
Click on Settings.

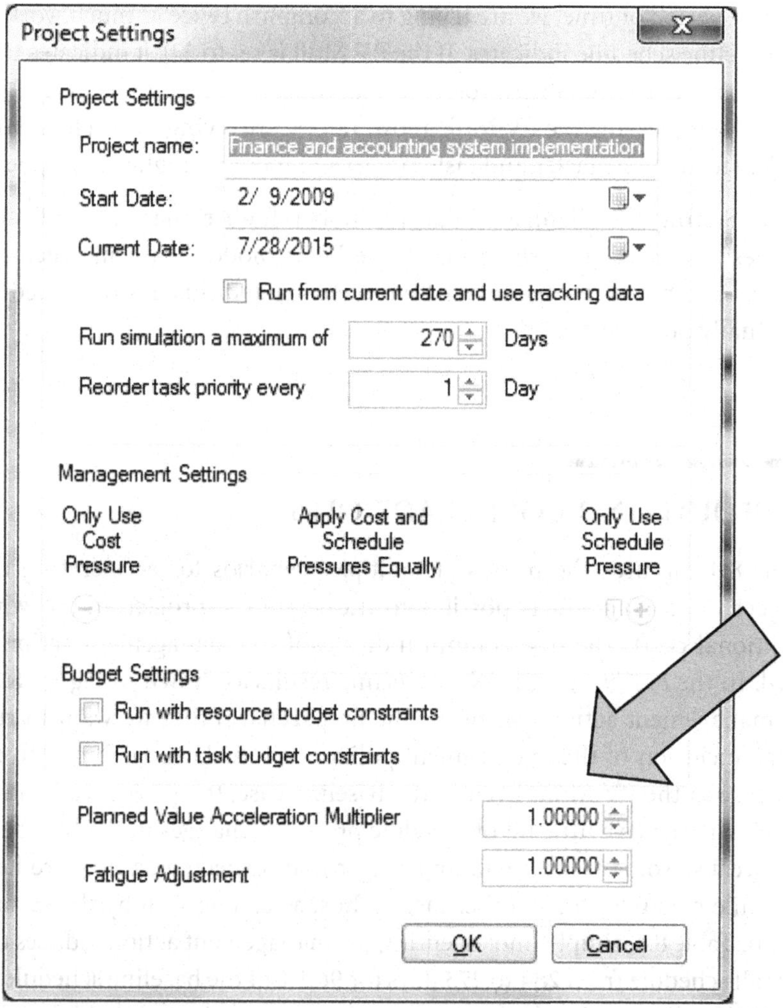

FIGURE 8.21
PV Mult and Fatigue Adjustment.

The PV Mult is the driver of the acceleration analysis. All the other inputs so far have set up the pmBLOX project file so that the appropriate management policy will kick in when it needs to, the resources are used according to the management policy, and the resources suffer productivity losses that are reasonable if worked OT for a significant amount of time.

Referring back to the earned value overview in Chapter 4, the planned value is the expected budget at the end of the project (typically measured in cost but could also be measured as resource hours). Setting the PV Mult to 2.0 indicates trying to get the project done in half the time (50% schedule).

For any period of time, we are trying to accomplish twice as much work as the baseline schedule indicates. If the PV Mult is set to 3.0, it indicates that we are trying to finish the project in one-third of the original time. And so on. By increasing the PV Mult above 1.0, we are trying to accelerate the project to get done faster and faster (with a higher and higher multiplier).

Note: Setting the Planned Value Multiplier higher than 1.0 indicates the desire to accelerate the project. The DPM model (with management actions and productivity impacts) will determine if this desired schedule is actually possible.

SCHEDULE AND COST TRADE-OFFS

Table 8.4 captures the results of multiple scenarios for accelerating the project (or, seeing if it is possible to accelerate the project and at what additional cost). The first column indicates if the management action is used. In the *baseline* pmBLOX case (same results as shown in Figure 8.3), no management action was used. The first scenario that we want to run is the inclusion of the management policy with the baseline but with no increase in the PV Mult. Even in the baseline case, the project can some-times experience a little bit of schedule pressure (changes in the SPI) sim-ply because some tasks are taking longer than expected as they are held up while resources finish other tasks. Thus, as can be seen by the second row in Table 8.4, simply implementing the management action reduces the overall schedule from 284 to 273 days (or 96.1% of the baseline schedule in pmBLOX). But, notice that the cost for this scenario is slightly higher due to the higher cost of OT hours for some of the resources (as shown in Table 8.1) as well as very slight productivity losses due to fatigue from working a little bit of OT. The total cost is now $302,564, with $22,644 of that cost coming from OT work.

The remaining rows in Table 8.4 try to push the project faster and faster to get a shorter and shorter schedule. Thus, the PV Mult gets higher values. The third column of Table 8.4 shows the desired schedule performance based on the PV Mult. The fourth column in Figure 8.4 shows the actual schedule performance (when productivity impacts are included). On the third row of Table 8.4, the PV Mult is 1.25, which indicates that we are try-ing to finish the project in 80% of its baseline schedule (i.e., 1/1.25 = 0.80).

TABLE 8.4

Project Acceleration Scenarios

Mgt Actions?	PV Mult	Desired Schedule (% of Baseline)	Actual Schedule (% of Baseline)	Cost (% of Baseline)	Duration (Days)	Regular Hours Cost	OT Hours Cost	Total Cost
No	1.00	100%	0.0%	0.0%	284	$288,867	$—	$288,867
Yes	1.00	100%	96.1%	104.7%	273	$279,910	$22,654	$302,564
Yes	1.25	80%	81.3%	107.3%	231	$232,695	$77,140	$309,835
Yes	1.50	67%	71.5%	115.9%	203	$214,037	$120,719	$334,756
Yes	2.00	50%	70.1%	134.2%	199	$217,688	$169,891	$387,579
Yes	4.00	25%	67.3%	160.2%	191	$221,721	$240,942	$462,664
Yes	10.00	10%	70.1%	166.8%	199	$229,288	$252,443	$481,730

We almost get there with an actual schedule of 81.3% of the baseline schedule but with a cost impact of 107.3% (i.e., 7.3% higher than the baseline). This continues through the rest of the scenarios in the table until the final scenario in which the PV Mult = 10, and we are trying to finish the project in only 10% of its baseline schedule. Notice that in this case, with PV Mult = 10, the project can only get to 70.1% of the baseline schedule, not the desired 10%.

A picture is worth a thousand words, so consider Figure 8.22. Everything in this book comes down to this graphic to demonstrate the power of using the DPM instead of the CPM. The first thing to observe is that the more the project is accelerated, the less likely the project will reach the desired schedule (as shown in the third and fourth columns of Table 8.4). And, the more the project is accelerated, the greater the OT use and the higher the total cost. Also, looking at the points in Figure 8.22 (and the corresponding estimated relationship curve), it is clear to see that there is a theoretical shortest possible duration for this project based on the resources available, the task relationships, and the single management action. Of course, other management actions could be implemented, such as adding resources when behind schedule, and additional resources could be made available. This would result in a different curve and a different theoretical shortest

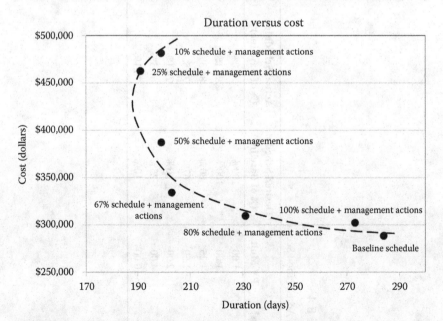

FIGURE 8.22
Cost and schedule trade-offs from scenarios.

possible duration. However, the concept is the same, and so this simple example of a single management action based on OT hours is enough to have the discussion.

Figure 8.22 shows several important dynamics that project planners and managers need to know:

- *There are cost consequences that are associated with accelerated schedules.* As stated numerous times throughout this book, the simple CPM approach cannot show this. The schedule (duration) can be arbitrarily set by the project manager in the tool, and the cost will never increase, as evidenced in the defense sector example in Figure 1.1. No matter what the schedule is, a CPM-based tool will simply add up the normal cost of the resources.

- *The relationship between schedule and cost is not linear.* In CPM-based tools, when work backlog is accounted for (e.g., effort-driven tasks in Microsoft Project), the assumption is that the schedule can linearly decrease. By doubling the resources, the duration can be cut in half. By doubling the work hours, the duration can be cut in half. In the real world, this is absolutely not true in most cases. Furthermore, the relationship between the reduction in schedule and the resulting additional costs is typically never linear. It is almost always nonlinear.

- *It is entirely possible to push a project too hard such that the productivity losses are high enough that the project not only costs more but also takes longer.* This is seen in the Mythical Man-Month example that is cited in Chapter 1. On software projects, if additional developers are used to try to get a late project back on schedule, the project takes longer (as the experienced resources have to assist the new resources and fix new bugs that are introduced) and costs more (because we are now paying for additional resources).

While most project managers (especially experienced ones) know these dynamics to be true, until now, there has been no method for incorporating these dynamics into common project planning and management tools. Thus, we have limped along using an old and outdated method: CPM. Even if the tool is available over the Internet with various bells and whistles, 60-year-old technology is still 60-year-old technology. The DPM finally provides a method for understanding and quantifying these dynamics, and it gives project planners and managers a level of realism that will improve their cost and schedule estimates as well as their abilities to manage projects (by testing various management policies). The end result is higher project success rates. Essentially, project planning is not as easy as some of the current CPM-based tools would have us believe. The simplicity of the CPM will hurt the project and decrease the probably of project success. The movement to agile and lean methods in project management have attempted to address some of these deficiencies by adding the concept of product work/feature backlogs. This is exactly what the DPM builds upon. Work needs to be done, and resources are the means for getting work done. If this is not captured in the methodology and algorithms employed in our project planning and management tools, we are severely limited in our ability to establish a realistic and achievable plan.

Please visit http://www.dynamicprogressmethod.com and http://www.pmblox.com for more information and examples.

Index

Printed in the United States
by Baker & Taylor Publisher Services